Contents

8 • Contents

6/30/17
$15.95

Advance Praise

"A chasm of distrust lies wedged between religious and secular world views, preventing meaningful dialogue and sustainable engagement. Often, those who make the journey from religion to secularism are scathing in their indictment of those left behind. Drew Bekius refuses that course. The story around which he built his life crashes around him with cinematic drama. But standing in the wreckage, he draws on a strength of commitment he learns is all his own, and turns it to the work of building dialogue. In an extraordinary offering, Bekius invites those on both sides of the chasm to find their way toward one another and, as they do so, to build an alternative to rancour and a path toward understanding."

—Gretta Vosper, Minister at West Hill United Church of Toronto

"Drew Bekius has written a clear, engaging, and thought-provoking book about finding faith and losing it. Along the way, he addresses fellow skeptics, believers, and everyone in between as he uses his own story to explore what it means to move in and out of organized religion. *The Rise and Fall of Faith* is a deep, satisfying, and ultimately hopeful read. I highly recommend it for those seeking to express their differences and find common ground among those with whom they disagree."

—Katherine Ozment, author of *Grace Without God: The Search for Meaning, Purpose, and Belonging in a Secular Age*

"This book is not an analysis, not a takedown, not a manifesto. It's personal. After a high school prayer launched Drew Bekius into 'missionary zeal' and eventually the ministry, a questioning mind brought it all crashing down—and he was left to decide what to do with the pieces. Watching him assemble those fragments into bridges that bring people together makes for a gratifying and memorable read."

—Dale McGowan, Founder of Foundation Beyond Belief

"The journey out of religion is often difficult, much more so for those who dedicated their lives to a religion. As a recovering minister, Drew's story is compelling and inspiring. I could not put it down. For understanding and inspiration, read *The Rise and Fall of Faith*."

—Darrel Ray, Founder of Recovering from Religion

"This polarized country of ours needs more leaders like Drew Bekius, who are willing to tell their transition stories without trashing the people and traditions they leave behind. Drew certainly doesn't soft peddle how difficult his deconversion was, but he doesn't make finding meaning, purpose, and a sense of belonging on the other side of faith seem like an impossible ordeal either. In the end, his new book offers both hope and practical ideas to humanists like me, who want to stay close to our Christian friends and family members while proactively pursuing goodness in an openly secular way."

—Bart Campolo, Humanist Chaplain at the University of Southern California

"An enjoyable read, *The Rise and Fall of Faith* quickly captivates the reader and takes them along on Bekius's wonderful journey of thought through a path strewn with valuable insights. Humanity would be in a better place if we all stopped to examine our own flaws and contradictions and endeavor to discover better answers for our questions about life. Bekius's empowering postfaith embrace of humanism uplifts the reader as the potential for joy founded in honest reality is revealed."

—Roy Speckhardt, Executive Director of the American Humanist Association

"This is a joy to read. It's written in a breezy style that makes it easy to keep reading. With humor, sincerity, and openness, the author tells the reader how he resolves the very serious issues he faces as his religious faith grows, becomes a powerful force in his life, then wanes and eventually ends."

—Linda LaScola, coauthor of *Caught in the Pulpit: Leaving Belief Behind*

"Drew Bekius tells his personal story of a church providing content and meaning in his difficult teenage years and a channel for his zeal as a young pastor. These are useful roles for churches. As Drew discovered, churches should learn to do these things without spouting false 'facts.' Drew leads a Christian reader through his own awakening to flaws in biblical literalism. Christians will likely find it compelling. Drew's personal story of losing his life as he lost his faith and yet surviving is a compelling read that will resonate for others doubting their faith."

—Jeff T. Haley, lead author of *Sharing Reality: How to Bring Secularism and Science to an Evolving Religious World*

"For many people their loss of religious faith causes a mild disruption in their lives. Maybe they have to find a new social circle. Maybe they avoid the topic at family gatherings, or compromise with a still-religious spouse. But for Drew Bekius his loss of faith and embrace of atheism shattered the world he thought he knew and his place in it. Drew sacrificed his livelihood, family, and very reason for living when his logical mind could no longer contain the contradictions and fallacies of faith. That journey is described in direct, honest prose by a man who went from (proverbial) hell and back to find joy in the true nature of reality—one without a Jesus bestie. This book is for anyone who is looking to understand the evangelical mind and why breaking from facially absurd dogma requires more than just clear thinking. It requires courage."

—Robyn Blumner, President and CEO of the Center for Inquiry

THE RISE
AND FALL
OF FAITH

*A God-to-Godless Story
for Christians and Atheists*

DREW BEKIUS

FOREWORD BY DAN BARKER

Pitchstone Publishing
Durham, North Carolina

Pitchstone Publishing
Durham, North Carolina
www.pitchstonepublishing.com

Portions of this book were originally published as blog posts at DrewBekius.com.

10 9 8 7 6 5 4 3 2 1

Library of Congress Cataloging-in-Publication Data

Names: Bekius, Drew, author.
Title: The rise and fall of faith : a God-to-Godless story for Christians and
    atheists / Drew Bekius ; foreword by Dan Barker.
Description: Durham, North Carolina : Pitchstone Publishing, 2017. | Includes
    bibliographical references.
Identifiers: LCCN 2016057467| ISBN 9781634311106 (pbk. : alk. paper) |
ISBN
    9781634311120 (epdf) | ISBN 9781634311137 (mobi)
Subjects: LCSH: Bekius, Drew. | Ex-clergy—United States—Biography. |
    Ex-church members—United States—Biography. | Atheists—United
    States—Biography. | Atheism—United States. | Christianity and atheism.
Classification: LCC BL2790.B45 b A3 2017 | DDC 211/.8092 [B] —dc23
LC record available at https://lccn.loc.gov/2016057467

for Janett and Jocelyn

Foreword

"Welcome to the secret life of Pastor Drew."

I remember that god-awful feeling. Standing in a pulpit before a congregation of smiling Christians in southern California in the summer of 1983, I experienced the same "glitch" that Drew Bekius describes almost three decades later. As the words I was preaching rolled over that audience, I heard the people say "Amen" and "Praise the Lord" and "Thank you, Jesus." But my own mind was saying, "Wait a minute." I was just becoming convinced that what I used to believe "with all my heart and all my soul and all my mind and all my strength" was surprisingly and painfully not true after all. And if Christianity was a fake, so was I. For almost twenty years I had proclaimed the truth of Jesus with supreme confidence, but now the words I was pushing out of my mouth sounded awkward and embarrassing, like a bad joke that makes you want to cringe instead of laugh.

As I describe in my book *Godless*, after one of those sermons, during those few months of hypocrisy before I figured out how to break my preaching off for good, a woman came up to me and said, "Reverend Barker, I want you to know that I really felt the spirit of God on your ministry tonight." I was stunned. How could she sense from me what I was not feeling myself? I had been afraid that those "spirit-led" believers would have discerned the phoniness and hollowness I was experiencing.

But, of course, they didn't. That woman's remarks confirm that something else is going on, something other than what we all believed was happening. Worshippers are not "in the spirit." There is no spirit. They are really "in the psychology."

But that was not an easy lesson to learn, not for someone who had been trained to "bring into captivity every thought to the obedience of Christ," who had loudly and proudly proclaimed the saving grace of Jesus. Drew Bekius learned this astonishing truth much like I did. The hard way. "Trying to make sense of what doesn't make sense will make you crazy," Drew writes. I can say "Amen" to that. It can drive you nuts trying to pound the square peg of faith into the round hole of reality. The simple solution, which was impossible to spot at the time, I can now clearly view in hindsight. Throw away the peg! Let reality be reality.

Well, that is easy to say, but for an ordained minister who has dedicated his or her entire life to the ministry, it is worse than blasphemy. *The Rise and Fall of Faith* tells the gripping story of one preacher who overcame the inertia and steered his way to sanity. Like me, Drew Bekius finally became that new creature of which the biblical writers so ignorantly wrote. Atheism is not the cure for the disease of faith. It is the prevention.

The only thing we truly own is our story. Everything else can be taken away. Drew possesses a precious story, one that you will truly enjoy reading. Although his specific journey is unique in so many amazing ways, the general path he took, while still rare, is not unique. Hundreds of other ministers have made the same escape, but when I came out of the pulpit, I did not know of a single story like mine. I thought I was all alone. Working with the Freedom From Religion Foundation (FFRF), I eventually encountered a handful of other preachers and priests who had abandoned the supernatural. At FFRF's 1985 convention in Minneapolis (when Drew Bekius was in kindergarten an hour's drive away), four former clergymen—Baptist preacher Delos McKown, Episcopal priest Dick Hewetson, liberal Baptist minister Charlie French, and I, an evangelical pastor— formed a panel (perhaps the first of its kind) to compare stories about leaving the ministry. Today we have The Clergy Project, with currently more than seven hundred ministers, priests, rabbis, imams, nuns, and other ordained religious professionals (some still in the pulpit) who have become atheists or agnostics. We have books by former clergy such as *Out of God's Closet* by Stephen Uhl, *Writing God's Obituary* by Anthony Pinn, *Why I Became an Atheist* by John Loftus, *Farewell to God* by John Templeton, *Hope After Faith* by Jerry DeWitt, *From Apostle to Apostate* by Catherine Dunphy, *To the Cross and Back* by Fernando Alcántar, *Towards the Light* by John Compere, *One Nun's Odyssey* by Marion Kenneally, *The Ebony Exodus Project* by Candace Gorham, *The Rector Who Wouldn't Pray for Rain* by Pat Semple, *Life Beyond Belief* by Bob Ripley, *With Faith and Fury* (a semi-autobiographical novel) by Delos McKown, my own books *Losing Faith in Faith* and *Godless*, and many more listed at ClergyProject.org, including the stories in *Caught in The Pulpit* by Daniel C. Dennett and Linda LaScola.

And now we have *The Rise and Fall of Faith*, by Drew Bekius, perhaps the most candid and witty account of a reverend on the run. It is unpretentious, deadly serious, and jaw-droppingly funny in places. While reading it, I chuckled out loud at the incongruity and irony. This is no atheist sermon; it is a searingly honest human confession.

Each person who leaves the ministry tells their own tale, but I have noticed a common theme. We are all readers. The only way I could "Google" in the early 1980s was to devour every book I could lay my hands on. Drew Bekius, who includes his own reading list here, tells a similar story. So does Carter Warden, a conservative Church of Christ minister from Tennessee who came out publicly as an atheist at FFRF's 2016 convention in Pittsburgh, after an agonizing seven and a half years (!) trapped as a nonbeliever in the pulpit before he could find a good exit strategy. During his speech, Carter emphasized the list of sixty books he had read during his journey to honesty. Clearly, we apostates did not take the decision to leave the ministry lightly. We needed to be look-before-you-leap certain before throwing away the precious years we had devoted to the "good news" of heaven and hell. We want to build our house on the rock, not the sand.

My story is thirty years older than Drew's, but I am surprised at the similarities. Like me, Drew was something of a "Jesus nerd." Unlike most of our Christian friends, we took our faith super seriously. We both felt called to the ministry as teenagers, graduated from conservative Christian colleges, and preached for about the same amount of time. We were each around the age that Jesus allegedly died when our faith in Jesus died. Although biblical contradictions were not the most important problem for other former clergy (especially for the more liberal types), they were extremely troublesome to conservative evangelicals like Drew and me. "If the Bible can't get this stuff right," he writes, "then we have a serious challenge toward its accuracy and therefore its credibility." Like me, Drew has many pleasant memories of his religious life and writes with true affection about some of his Christian friends and relatives. Neither of us had read a single atheist book before we became atheists. We did our own thinking—which is what everyone should do. Drew's story, like mine, includes a traumatic life-threatening "atheist in a foxhole" emergency, after which we realized we felt no need to pray during the entire frightening but strangely peaceful episode. Instead of invoking the supernatural, we invoked the best medical care we could find. And just like

Drew tells it—what former Louisiana pastor Jerry DeWitt also says in *Hope After Faith*—I can confirm that when you discard the shackles of dogma, authentic joy follows. True happiness arises not from submission, but from the freedom to live and think for yourself. Like one of my songs says, "Life is unbelievably good!"

The Rise and Fall of Faith contains a wealth of revelation. Bekius has provided "think outside the box" study questions for each chapter that focus on what matters, but for me the two most important take-home messages of this book are authenticity and integrity.

"You were never a true Christian in the first place," I often hear, "or you would never have rejected someone so powerful, loving, and real as Jesus." However, after reading this book, nobody will dare say Drew Bekius was "just pretending." If he was not a true Christian, nobody is. He gave God (while he believed in him) every opportunity to make himself real. Trusting that "all things whatsoever you shall ask in my name believing, you shall receive," he prayed in the name of Jesus, asking for assurance. He wept, and prayed even more. He was not looking for an excuse to abandon Christianity so that he could live a selfish life. He *wanted* it to be true. He *believed* it was true. He *lived* as if it were true. He studied the scriptures diligently. He spent serious time alone in humble reflection and aching yearning for the love of Christ. He sought counsel from wiser Christian mentors. He met regularly with pastoral peer groups where he aired his honest questions in the spirit of learning and growing stronger in the faith. As much as is humanly possible, he lived a blameless, moral, obedient, God-fearing life. Long after his faith had frayed beyond recognition—much longer than any normal mortal would hang on—he kept praying! He wanted it to work. The last thing he wanted was to become a godless heathen.

You can't always get what you want. But if you try sometimes, you just might find you get what you need.

What Drew desperately needed was integrity. When you finish this book, you will rejoice with me that he finally got it!

The next time you see a preacher or a priest, remember this: they are just people. Although most members of the clergy are good human beings, they don't have any special edge. If they did, they would not disagree with each other (contrary to the Apostle Paul's admonition "that all of you be in agreement and that there be no divisions among you, but that you be united in the same mind and the same purpose"). They are not smarter or kinder than you. They don't have any spooky pipeline to truth. Even though their motives may be sincere, all of them (even those who do not admit it) have doubts and insecurities. Be patient with them. They are doing the best they can, but they can do better. Perhaps after reading this book, some of them will.

—**Dan Barker**
    Freedom From Religion Foundation
    Madison, Wisconsin

Author's Note

There can be some debate over the definition of an *atheist*. The common definition is the one embraced in this book, where the *a-* prefix negates the meaning found in the rest of the word. So just as a *theist* is one who possesses belief in the existence of a god or gods, so an *atheist* is simply one who *doesn't* possess belief in the existence of a god or gods. As such, atheism is not a belief set of its own but rather is simply a term that identifies one's *lack* of belief. This is how I use the term throughout this book.

When discussing Christianity and Christians, my primary frame of reference is evangelicalism, a conservative Christian movement—slightly more mainstream than fundamentalism—that holds firmly to the idea that its Bible is the inspired and error-proof Word of God. I fully realize that Christianity is diverse and that not all Christians hold the Bible as inspired by God. Nonetheless, many of the questions I ask of "believing Christians" assume an evangelical perspective in keeping with my personal experiences and the context of the book.

Unless otherwise noted, all direct Bible quotes are from *The Holy Bible: English Standard Version* (Crossway, 2002), the rendition of choice within many evangelical Christian circles. For more information, see John Piper's January 1, 2004 post "Good English With Minimal Translation: Why Bethlehem [Church] Uses the ESV" (http://www.desiringgod.org/articles/good-english-with-minimal-translation-why-bethlehem-uses-the-esv).

Finally, the events I portray in this book are to the best of my memory and understanding, which of course may be different from the memory and understanding of others. Similarly, statements and words I ascribe either to myself or others in the book all come from my own recollections. Thus, they do not represent exact transcripts but rather serve to evoke the feeling and meaning of what I heard or said over the course of my journey into and out of faith.

Prologue

It was the afternoon of Thursday, March 26, 2015. I was on the campus of the Moody Bible Institute of Chicago and sitting with a seminary student named Mike. Ten years earlier I had served on pastoral staff at the fairly large Chicago church where Mike and his family were active participants. I knew him and his family well. And now Mike was attending Moody Theological Seminary and acquiring an M.A. in Clinical Mental Health Counseling.

Meanwhile, those ten years had seen me take the next in my ever-ongoing series of evangelical Christian adventures. For nearly twenty years I had lived and breathed nothing but Jesus. From ages fifteen to thirty-three, I followed "Him" as hard as I could with everything I had. The sojourn of faith had consumed my entire life as I devoted every waking breath to the pleasure and service of the King of Kings. And it was more than exciting. It was rich with majesty and wonder. It was intimately personal, adamantly hopeful, and saturated with purpose. Eventually I followed the call of Jesus into pastoral ministry, where I served him tirelessly for twelve years at two churches, first at Mike's church and then at the one that followed.

But then something began to change.

As those years trudged on, as I continued on my journey, I grew increasingly plagued by the reality that my faith had fallen short of all it had promised, troubled by the realization that this lacking had been covered up by an endless circle of shallow explanations and trite responses. The more I noticed, the less I could deny . . . and the more the unraveling of my faith revealed its hollowed center.

And eventually the word had spread to Mike and the rest of my former congregants.

I had become an atheist.

And here we find ourselves in the early months of 2015, where our young evangelical seminarian studying Christian clinical counseling was assigned a group project that would eventually bring him to the intersection where I was standing. And in the process, his project pulled me back to my very own alma mater, where I sat, coffee in hand, before a rolling video camera.

The challenge of Mike's class was to create Christian therapists who were able to counsel clients without letting personal bias get in the way of providing genuine assistance, even if it meant setting aside their own personal religious views. Each group was to select a segment of the population markedly unlike its group members and consider what it would be like to provide them treatment. *What would it take to understand such a client's perspective, to see the world as they see it, and to therefore enter into it and counsel them as they attempt to navigate their lives in truly beneficial and meaningful ways?* Each student cluster selected its own demographic to study. Mike's group chose atheists.

That's when I received a text message from Mike asking if I still remembered him.

And that's when just a few weeks later, we sat down for our nearly two-hour interview on everything from common misconceptions and societal challenges atheists face to the reasons an atheist might willingly choose to see a Christian counselor. *Honestly,* I told Mike, *it's hard for me to envision an atheist* ever *actively choosing an overtly Christian counselor instead of a secular one.* But maybe that was beside the point.

But before Mike and I spent any time talking about all this stuff, he first asked me to share my story, the story of how I had become an unbeliever. Mike then went on to ask about the influences that had led me to atheism, about the books I had read or the other atheists that had gotten me thinking in that direction. I shared with Mike how, prior to my deconversion from Christianity, I hadn't read a single book on atheism by a single atheist author. I shared how there wasn't even one single atheist friend who had challenged my thinking and gotten me going. And I shared how the number one book prodding me to question and reevaluate my beliefs was, of all things, the Christian Bible.

And it was then, about a quarter of the way through the interview, after I had shared my story and dismantled the system of influences that he had been taught to assume, when my interviewer released the most insightful comment made the entire day. After this particular question, Mike turned his camera off and took a step back, starring slightly off to the side and apparently out the window. His eyes widened, his head tilted to the side, and even as he still seemed to be processing the syllables falling from his mouth, Mike said: *"Wow, this disproves everything we normally believe about atheism."*

He paused again, stared through the floor for a moment, and after attempting to rein in his thoughts, looked up, turned the camera back on, and returned to the business of the interview.

What you have in your hands is more than just my story. It is a bridge to understanding. And like all bridges, it extends both ways. To any atheists in the room, it may seem clear that Christians (and other religionists alike) hold many false assumptions about nonbelievers. Just one of which—and it can often seem a foundational one at that—is the declaration that a former Christian could never have actually been a "true" Christian to begin with. It comes from this Calvinist theological belief called Perseverance of the Saints and is often referred to with the tagline "Once Saved, Always Saved."

This idea stems from the belief that true Christians are those who have experienced the right kind of "saving faith," which has led to a supernatural transformation wielded by the Holy Spirit of God—*the equivalent of saying God Himself*—and once God wields such a fundamental reconstruction of the individual, it cannot be undone. Therefore, if anyone ever proclaims that they have forsaken Christ, clearly their faith was never actually transformative to begin with. Once saved, always saved. And so if Drew is an atheist today, we can know for sure that he was never truly a Christian in the first place.

Or so the thinking goes.

That's just one assumption often made of atheists by Christians. But there are others. That they are immoral. That they just want an excuse to sin. That they are mad at God. That they are bitter and angry. Or maybe that they're just sad and lonely and destined to walk the earth without a valid sense of purpose. Some equate atheists with Satanists. Others with Communists. Or they simply believe atheism to be a force that threatens to undermine the very fabric of human civilization itself.

But maybe the biggest false assumption of them all is that a flourishing and fulfilling, committed and devout, Bible-centered faith could never lead to complete disbelief all on its own. And as we're about to discover in the chapters that lie ahead, this assertion is most patently false.

In my story, I will walk you step-by-step along the journey I have taken. You will see what I saw and feel what I felt as my faith built to the point of being completely "sold out" for Jesus. Those of faith can compare my thoughts and feelings with their own to see how they hold up and judge for themselves, if they so dare, whether or not the state of my simple childlike faith was genuine. But you will then also discover what it looks like for a committed and zealous evangelical pastor to lose his faith even as he works tirelessly each and every day to hold it in check, even as its final grains slip as sand through his tightly gripped fingers. In so doing, you will peer into the heart and mind of a moment-by-moment crisis of faith.

But the bridge truly does extend both ways. And the truth is that atheists may be prone to making just as many assumptions about Christians, specifically those of the evangelical variety, of which I represent. Some, for instance, might find it odd that an evangelical seminary would even attempt to train their student therapists in how to set aside religious bias in an effort to provide nonbelievers with genuine help. Some might assume there have to be ulterior motives behind the "unbiased" therapy. Others might be shocked to even hear of such an institution embracing mainstream psychology to begin with.

And this says nothing of the political assumptions normally made of Christians—that all evangelicals are presumably fused with the Religious Right and its Grand Old Party of Republicans. And so it may be surprising to learn of the fact that while a student in the very institution mentioned above, I was first challenged by professors to consider voting Democrat and that while employing the very framework I picked up here, I decided to help elect Senator Barack Obama to the presidency. You wouldn't necessarily expect to find room for such perspectives within evangelical Christianity, let alone from one of its own pastors trained at one of the world's flagship Bible colleges. But this is just a shadow of the misconceptions often made of evangelicals. And here they were all confronted in just one brief story in the prologue of many more to come.

Now I suppose you could say that if it's worth writing about something and worth reading about it, then it's also worth using it to provoke a discussion. I'd love to think maybe—*just maybe*—this little pile of ramblings might give us cause to do more of this very thing. That it might give *you* cause to engage in such discussion yourself.

I suppose you could say that the fundamental purpose of this book is to take you inside the heart and mind of an evangelical pastor in the midst of losing is faith. *What does he see? What does he feel? What are his thoughts and struggles?*

And what would the story look like if he were you?

Even more fundamentally, my hope is that we would all ask ourselves: *What would YOU see and hear and taste and feel? What would be YOUR sticking points? And what about your BREAKING point? What would hold YOU together and keep YOU sane? And, most importantly, how can you really be sure, until you've been there yourself?*

More questions will come later. More discussion points. And, hopefully, more actual conversations fueled by this story and others like it. There are many. Some in print. Others via podcast. And for this reason, each chapter spills into a set of questions provided for dialogue. Some of them are aimed specifically at Christian readers, others at atheists, but all are offered in an effort to get us thinking and talking more directly. And in conversation with one another.

So anyway, welcome to my story.

And welcome to your own. Even if for no other reason than that your story includes you reading mine. But it's not just the story of yours and mine. It's the story of all humanity in our grand and epic search for meaning and truth and even for God Himself. It's the story of a searching people. And in this sense, it is most certainly a story much bigger than my own. It is *ours*.

Welcome to the Story of Faith.

PART ONE:
THE RISE OF THIS EVANGELICAL FAITH

Chapter One

The Gym-Kitchen Prayer That Changed My Life

Fifteen hours down. Eleven to go. Trying to catch a little sleep on the floor of a crowded bus is a tireless endeavor . . . Somehow my legs were cramping even as they were going numb. My twisted body tightly molded to the cold damp surface; it pressed around a forest of iron posts. The stench of sweat and stale Doritos steeped in the lingering fog from which I fought for breath. I begged the screeching drumbeat in my head to allow me even a couple hours' sleep, though I realized my slumber's greater threat was the compounding army of anticipations that raced for the repeated airtime on the big-screen amphitheater of my mind.

I opened my eyes. An epic relay of illuminations formed a dancing glow on the mangled chicken sandwich that lay just a few feet out of reach. I think that's when the orphaned football tottered down the aisle . . .

I found footing for my hands and pushed my torso one side over the other, pulling my legs from their pinned formation underneath the seat two rows back. Refashioning my folded jacket, I settled my head once more under the seat in front of me as the sheath of stubborn vinyl flooring pressed itself through my makeshift pillow. I closed my eyes and returned to the kaleidoscope of future memories as our youth group's charter bus churned diligently through twilight acreage. Saint Cloud, Minnesota to Washington, DC.

And here is where my story begins.

On a charter bus stuffed with teenagers and their overly eager chaperones. The year was 1994 and it was only about a month before the freshman portion of my high school experience was set to begin. I was on my way to what had been billed as a "peer evangelism super-conference." And it was surely going to be a big deal. Organized by an influential group of evangelicals called Youth for Christ, the *super*-conference was designed to get believing high schoolers so excited about Jesus that their obsession with him would spread through social circles as effortlessly and organically as an *American Top 40* radio hit or a must-have pair of Girbaud jeans. References would be made toward *contagious Christianity*, that when our faith is healthy it spreads like a pro-life God virus that saves instead of harms, rescuing the entire world from the grips of hell. And in this effort, the conference promised to supply the training and tools needed to get teens especially serious about a lifestyle of evangelism—that is to say, about the development of their Jesus excitement and of sharing that excitement with others.

Anyway, I was one of about twenty kids from my home church, located in the small central Minnesota town of Milaca—*joined by what felt like about 178 other kids from other Saint Cloud–area churches*—all packed together in a stuffy bus on our way to Washington, DC. There, we would attend the conference and get really excited about this evangelism stuff and the sharing of our contagious Christian faith with others.

The name of the super-conference was DC/LA '94. The event was so named because it took place in two locations, with the other being way on the other side of the country in the City of the Angels, or, as they say in Spanish, Los Angeles.

You could say the real meat of the five-day event was its robust schedule of hundreds of training seminars and workshops. But like so many message-based gatherings, what drew the most attention was its nightly concerts with big-name headliner bands and a barrage of bestselling authors and motivational speakers. Or, at least they were big names within the evangelical community. If you'd spent any time in that world during the mid-1990s, you likely knew their names well, including DC Talk, Petra, and the Newsboys, and Josh McDowell, Tony Campolo, and the family-friendly comic Ken Davis. They were all there, along with more than twenty others. On top of this, a "True Love Waits" rally for sexual abstinence was planned for that Saturday afternoon on the National Mall. DC/LA '94—or at least the DC part—promised to be the most epic Jesus event of the year.

But to be perfectly honest, when I first signed up I was much more interested in a parent-free week's vacation than in a religious-training seminar. This would be the farthest from home that my limited travels had taken me. And I didn't have much of a social life, even by junior high standards, so the idea of spending a week traveling the country and hanging out with a group of high schoolers who were all much cooler than I was beyond exhilarating. It was a fantasy-perfect mid-July getaway.

So that night as our bus trekked its way to the capital, my ability to catch a few hours' sleep didn't stand a chance against the anticipations churning within my head. The imaginative flow was rather ceaseless as my mind found it more than a little difficult to power down. There were just a few too many expectations burning for fuel. Yet even in the ceaseless flow of vibrant dreams, I really had no idea just how much this conference was about to change my life.

When we arrived at our budget-friendly motel, we discovered that our reservation was one of many lost in the previous week's power outage. But there was good news. Our would-be motel scrambled to fix the situation by finding accommodations elsewhere for all the lost reservation holders. As a result, our group found lodging at some place named the Stouffer Renaissance Mayflower Hotel.

Turned out that this place where we were about to stay was absolutely legendary. Built in 1792, it was known everywhere simply as The Mayflower and was regarded as the Grande Dame of Washington. A hotel of four stars and four diamonds, it wasn't merely rated one of the nation's top ten, but had been declared "The Hotel of Presidents."

Until then, my most thrilling hotel experiences had been Holiday Inn swimming pools. But here at The Mayflower we discovered rooms with imported Italian marble countertops and one of those cool minibars that up until then I had only seen in the movies. There was a closet filled with embroidered white robes made of the softest material I had ever previously touched, and one of the three telephones was located in the bathroom so you could order room service while sitting on a great porcelain throne. Here we were, with our week just getting started, and it was already the most exciting of my life.

Then we discovered an Israeli ambassador was staying in our building to work on the peace treaty with Jordan. *An ambassador and a peace treaty. In our building.* I'm not sure I really knew what any of that meant, but it sounded fascinating and certainly larger than anything my daily routine was fit to encounter.

So that first morning we roamed the hotel in search of the Grand Ballroom used for presidential inauguration parties. But along the way, our original agenda fell victim to the wonder of gilded ceilings and fine sculpture. Determined to take in every inch of millwork, our expedition eventually teased us up every button on the elevator.

But as doors opened to the tenth-story penthouse, a flood of Secret Service–looking agents lunged toward our elevator—with two of them then joining us inside. They talked into their wrists as they escorted us all the way down to the basement, where our departure was insisted upon. When we asked how we were to get back up to the lobby, they pointed toward the staircase to the side as the elevator doors closed between us and them. Wide-eyed as we were, we didn't mind the extra walk in the least. Each moment opened another fold in the map of an uncharted world.

Later that week, our elevator ride would be trumped by the glorious pomp of our Israeli friend's departing motorcade, a spectacle of power that burned a fantastic image in my mind that has remained ever since. This was not farmland Minnesota. And we were certainly not on this trip for the religious education alone.

But none of this stuff about Middle Eastern ambassadors or our stay at The Mayflower really had anything to do with what changed my life forever. Neither did our growing collection of Dream Team commemorative basketball cups picked up at every McDonald's along our trip. *Though I do believe I had seventeen of them by the end . . .*

No, to get to the part of the trip "that changed my life forever" we actually have to rewind our story a bit and back up to a few days before we even left for DC. I was sitting alone in the gymnasium kitchen of our small-town central Minnesota church reading through some of the conference's promotional materials—specifically, about all the techniques the conference promised to teach us as we won the world for Christ.

But what DC/LA '94 promised above all else was to light an inner fire within us.

It would infuse within our souls the desire and motivation needed to utilize these new tools, overcome our fears, and actively convince our friends to trust in Jesus. The conference would be nothing less than transformational. And the brochure glistened with its every word.

It all sounded great, I guess. The only problem was that as I read over all that was promised me, I didn't believe any of it.

Did I accept the theological need for evangelism, that it was up to us to get people saved by telling them about Christ? Yes. *Did I believe that many of my friends and family were otherwise bound for hell?* Yes. *Did I want them to accept Jesus and go to heaven?* Yes! I was an evangelical Bible-believing Christian, so *of course I did!*

But at the same time, the idea of talking to others about my faith seemed absolutely terrifying, and I didn't believe for a moment that there was anything a prepackaged program could do to change it.

See, I was kind of a nerd in junior high.

No, actually there's no *kind-of* about it. I was a total nerd, and I was the worst kind of a nerd. I was something of a *wannabe*. And honestly, I really truly deserved the moniker.

You know what a wannabe is. Someone who's "wanting to be" cool and trying way too hard to fit in with the popular crowd. Emphasize the words "trying way too hard." Well, that was me. And I was reminded of it every day of junior high.

As everyone gathered in the halls before school, I would go stand next to the cool kids. I would just stand there and silently search for something to say, something to contribute to the conversation. But not wanting to say something stupid, I usually just stood there without a word, looking dumb and feeling awkward. On occasion, I would make a brave move and stumble out something profound like *"Yeah"* or *"Exactly."* And it usually received a response of *"Hey, who asked you!! In fact, who gave this* wannabe *permission to even stand over here!? Get the hell outta here and go join the other dorks and losers!"*

But if nothing else, I was resilient. I didn't leave. Even when physically pushed to the side, I just stood there. Ignoring their request for permission papers, I looked to the floor and just hoped they would forget I was still there. Day after day and week after week. Year after year. I just couldn't go over to the other nerds and dorks. I honestly figured they'd just reject me as well, so if there was risk either way, I reasoned I might as well stay put. I didn't *want* to be known as a wannabe, but I did *wannabe* cool, and well, this kind of got me stuck in a rut that I couldn't quite figure my way out of.

Not that I didn't have any friends at all. I spent a bit of time with a couple kids from my church youth group. One of them, Bruce, would become a very close friend over the next couple years. We'd hang out regularly, pull pranks, make these comedic videos. Bruce had tons of friends and would one day be crowned homecoming king. But I wasn't good enough for them. Even my only friend's other friends blocked me from the rest of their circle.

But here's why I'm telling you all this: as I read the conference materials that afternoon, I knew within my soul that I could never jeopardize even the slightest chance at popularity, even if it was for the noble pursuit of saving souls. I just didn't have it in me. Being a religious nut would certainly add one more strike against my already lousy social reputation. I knew in my head that salvation was infinitely more important than a popularity contest, but I also knew that my heart and its ambitions were twisted out of alignment. As important as eternal things were, I couldn't escape how condemned my reputation would be if I started proselytizing to everybody. And yet I did genuinely want my family members and classmates to be in heaven with me. I just couldn't fathom having the inner strength to risk my own popularity to get them there.

So standing there that afternoon in the church's gym kitchen, I did it.

I stood there and prayed.

I prayed to God, and I dared him.

I laid out before God my dilemma, reminding him of what I understood to be his instructions and confessing my heart's simple unwillingness to follow orders. And then I dared him to change it. I literally prayed:

> *God, I* dare *you to use this conference to change this about me. I* want *the strength to tell people about Jesus, but I just don't think I ever could. I care too much about what they think of me, and the idea of sacrificing that is terrifying.* But I also want it to change. *If you are God, I dare you to show yourself in this way. I dare you to change me.*

I really did pray all of this. I also told him that I wasn't sure he could do it. That though I didn't necessarily think it *impossible* for him to spark such a change in my psyche, I also didn't expect it to happen. Yet nonetheless, I wanted it and challenged him to make it happen.

But I honestly didn't think he would. I moved on from that gymnasium kitchen and forgot about the prayer. I really did forget all about it. I went to the conference and never gave that gym-kitchen prayer a second thought. It wasn't until afterward that I saw connected dots.

In the years to follow I would view this as one of the most transformative prayers of my life. This experience would provide the foundation by which I would encourage others of faith to dare God to do big things. To look at the obstacles they faced, especially those they thought God unlikely to remove, and to challenge him to get up and do something. Don't be scared to dare God, I would say. He's a Big Boy. He can handle it.

As it turned out, I received everything promised by the super-conference on student evangelism. All the resources. And, more notably, all the motivation. Without even realizing it, throughout the week, day by day, all my fears were replaced with an impenetrable trust in God's bigger plan. I was placed "on mission" for Jesus. I tapped into an inner ravine of bold spiritual courage. And I discovered a greater thrill in striving as an ambassador of Christ than in striving to be cool enough for a beloved social circle. It didn't all materialize quite so literally overnight, but the building blocks fell into place just that quickly. The journey of discipleship had begun.

And all that I dared of God in that gym-kitchen prayer, he erupted upon my soul. Just two weeks after I came home from Washington, DC, I sat down with a guy from football practice to tell him he had to accept Jesus into his life. I was determined in my presentation, and I refused to take no for an answer. However, the interaction didn't go quite as I had planned. He didn't accept my invitation to faith right away. So I tried another angle. He refused again. Undeterred, I kept going. I railed and railed and railed until he gave in. But he never did. He instead ran from the meeting, cursing me as some sort of cult member. From then on, he maintained a physical distance from me throughout high school. But none of that mattered. Yes, his rejection was disappointing, but I felt invigorated by the fact that the rejection didn't suffocate me. I had become strong enough to care more about someone's eternity than about my own acceptance. And it felt transcendent. I felt invincible. The transformation of my life had begun.

Questions for the Dialogue

We're just beginning the story here and there's a lot more to come, but let's begin with a basic self-assessment.

For Everyone

- Take a moment to consider: Are you entering into this book with an open mind that is truly willing to extend the benefit of the doubt to the other side? Or are you simply here to justify your own preconclusions and looking for evidence to discredit your opponent? (Confidence in your perspective isn't necessarily bad, so be honest about your current state of mind.)

- Do you find yourself able to take the story at face value, trusting that events really happened as they are presented, or do you suspect the story has been adulterated in some way for the benefit of some ulterior motive? If the later, why?

For Believing Christians

- We already know that the young teen in this story is eventually going to become an atheist. In your opinion, does this discredit his faith as a teenager? If so, how?

- What is the best explanation for this teenager's prayer of confession and his "dare" to God? Do you feel it was genuine? And what is the best explanation for his sudden growth of boldness to tell his friends about Jesus? Was it answered prayer or possibly something else? What similarities might you find between his story and your own?

- Do you have preconceived notions about atheists? If so, are they positive or negative? What would it take to not automatically stereotype or assume the worst in an atheist?

For Atheists and Skeptics

- We already know that the young teen in this story is eventually going to become an atheist. How do you process his prayer "dare" to God and its apparent fulfillment? If God didn't answer that prayer, how could it appear as if he did?

- Do you feel the need to automatically assume the worst in the actions of all religious people, such as those who organized the conference? Do you find yourself looking for ulterior motives? If so, why?

- If you believed you knew the absolute truth about something, a truth that you believed could literally save lives, would you or would you not choose to share it? If so, why or why not?

- Do you have preconceived notions about Christians? If so, are they positive or negative? What would it take to not automatically stereotype or assume the worst in a Christian?

Chapter Two

Two More Prayers:
Building a Foundation for Faith

I had always been told that my spiritual journey began back in 1983. Within Christianity's evangelical and fundamentalist circles, everyone wants to know exactly when it was that you "got saved." And for those poor souls who aren't exactly sure how to answer that question, then the assumption is made that you were never a true believer to begin with.

In the minds of such Christians the most important prayer one can make is also the most foundational one, that crucial first step of faith, the one where a person places themselves before God, confesses their sin, asks forgiveness, and commits the rest of their lives to following the model and teachings of Jesus. It's the prayer that actually transforms a sinner into a true Christian. The day of this prayer becomes one's "spiritual birthday," forever looked back upon. Now, such a prayer commonly goes by various designations like "The Sinner's Prayer" or "The Prayer of Salvation," but most often it is known simply as "The Prayer." This prayer, *the* prayer, is the indisputable Big Kahuna. The very passageway into the Christian life itself.

And I prayed this prayer back in 1983, or so I am told. This was where, as a good little three-year-old boy attending a rural Baptist church, I sat one afternoon on the edge of the bathtub and followed my mother's lead. Hands were folded. Eyes closed tight. I formed my words after hers as I thanked Jesus for dying on the cross and asked him to come into my heart, forgive me my sins, and make me a new creation destined for heaven.

I suppose our theology might demand we credit that prayer as the truly transformational one in my life, but truth be told, I barely remember it. And though it was forever steeped with sentimentality, it didn't really seem to impact me in any noticeable way. I was, after all, only three years old.

Though I had always been told that my spiritual journey began back on that hallowed day, and though I am sure that in some larger environmental way this may be true, I think in reality, 1992 is the year it all started coming together, just a couple years prior to the Washington, DC trip.

Though my gym-kitchen prayer, as described in chapter one, may have been what launched my life of missionary zeal, there were two additional prayers that served to frame the faith of the young and ambitious Christian I was becoming. And, no, the prayer I uttered as a three-year-old wasn't one of them. No, the two other prayers that really filled in the gaps of my newly forming faith took place in the spring of 1992 and in the fall of 1996. This makes my gym-kitchen prayer the second of the three, the one in the middle.

But it's that first of the three to which we now turn . . .

Like many of life's little stories, I suppose this one starts off kinda sad, but thankfully it doesn't stay that way for long. I am told that I had had something of a somber childhood. Even though I never remembered it this way, apparently my mother first noticed signs of quiet sadness brewing within me as a young preschool boy. When she first shared these insights with me years later, I was honestly shocked. I have no recollection of depression until I was in the fifth grade. But in that fifth-grade year, oh man, sadness and despair set upon my mind and heart with brutal force.

And it was by the sixth grade that this sadness had grown into a deep depression that consumed each and every day, slowly drawing me to a point of emotional and spiritual breaking. I would go up to my bedroom and literally sob for hours. At times I found it difficult to breathe under the weight of despondency, my insides crushed by an overshadowing gloom. I grew so consumed with anger and bitterness that I would scream with strapped pillow to my face until the full volume of my lungs offered nothing more. I hated life, and the screams provided a momentary respite from the tension.

But truth be told, I really had no outwardly visible reason to be so upset and unsettled. I lived in a good home with a loving family, and all my needs were met. To this day my father remains a man of impenetrable integrity, built of the highest moral fiber. And if this book were about all the little life lessons I've learned throughout my years, this incredibly industrious man would fill nearly every page. My mother as well. Always loving, always there for me, she remains a great confidant to this day. I really truly had no apparent reason to be so damn sad.

And yet I absolutely detested my life and just about everything that intersected with it. I hated my breath. And my being. I wanted to die. And the fantasy of death was the ticking clock that ran every moment of my days. The metastasizing darkness overtook my will to live. Now this may sound intense and even a little overly dramatic, but I am not exaggerating when I tell you that every single day, I dreamt of slitting my wrists or swallowing pills or sneaking a shotgun.

Every. Single. Day.

Then came one Saturday afternoon in that spring of 1992, an afternoon that was a particularly difficult one. Holed up in my bedroom, drowning in a raging flood of tears and bitterness, it was more or less my usual rant. But *unusually* so, after an hour or two, my thoughts turned to God. This was rare since it was of course Saturday afternoon, not Sunday morning. But that's where they went. And my thoughts formed themselves into a prayer. I fashioned my feelings into a timeline of verbs and nouns that detailed to God the pain to which he seemed clearly an outsider. I itemized before him all the reasons I despised my pathetic and useless waste-of-space life.

And then I lamented the fact that despite all my efforts to think happy thoughts and focus on the positive, the sunshine never broke free of the cumulus. Even seeing the school social worker, who had helped a little, didn't really amount to much. And my mother told me I had to stop seeing her anyway. Nothing had helped. Nothing had relieved the pain. I was stuck in a deep dark chasm with no rope of rescue.

But that's when it hit me.

I had never asked God for help. Not really.

And so I decided to give him a try.

I cried out to him with a prayer that set my body aflame with goose bumps as I told him how much I truly needed him in my life. Now more than ever. With a great gust of Baptist informality, I told God that I was no longer sure anything could heal my depression, but that if there was any hope for healing, it had to be in him. I felt I had tried every other option and that God was the only one that remained. That afternoon, I asked him to return to me and to heal that which nothing else could. I pleaded with him to bring restoration to my soul and to rescue me from my great sadness.

I still find it astounding how instantaneous the response was. As I said, I had tried many forms of self-therapy that had all failed to lift my spirits, but in this prayer I felt a supernatural presence swirling about my head and around the room. As I breathed these words, I felt an immediate sense of comfort. For the first time in countless months, I felt a smile stretch upon my heart. Maybe my sense of introspection and self-awareness was a little more attuned than that of your typical twelve-year-old boy, but I was fully cognizant of these feelings and could see envisioned clouds vacating my soul. The inward deluge of tears receded and the spring season of joy bloomed forth. A warm front of calm welled up from within, and a deep sense of divine peace assured me that everything was going to be okay. The chaos was stilled. The turmoil subdued.

I smiled. I really smiled. I laughed. And it was a great big hearty laugh. My sense of normalcy had interweaved within itself a constant craving for death, but at this moment all desire to end my life was stripped away. One hundred percent gone. I no longer wanted to die. I knew God was with me, and I was overcome with a fantastic sense of confident hope. Everything was going to be okay. Everything *different*.

And in many ways it was. This isn't to say I left all sadness behind. Indeed, I've maintained something of a melancholy outlook most of my life. But all desire to end it with a *bang!* evaporated that day and did not return for several years, not even in the slightest.

I walked away from that sixth-grade afternoon with an unwavering confidence in the power of prayer. God had shown himself to me. Not physically, not visually or tangibly. But in the experience of spirit and emotion. And I would recount the glories of this day for the next two decades. I knew now that God was real and alive and active. That he was personal and compassionate. And that there was this mystical sense about the manifestation of his presence. It was this God that I would have the courage to *dare* two years later in our church's gym kitchen. He could move the mountains of within. And he was to be taken seriously.

Now fast-forward to that fall of 1996. It was here in this third and final of my three prayers where I learned how much God loves to bless his children with good gifts.

And this gift in particular was of the, shall we say, *romantic* variety.

Ready the rose petals and handwritten poetry . . .

Now by the time the eleventh grade had rolled around, and thanks to my ministry successes credited to my 1994 prayer dare, my social status as a wannabe had been eclipsed by a new unrivaled role. In the span of those two years, I had become the school's "preacher boy." This means, of course, that I was still mocked and ridiculed by most of the student body, but I was also being slowly held up by a select handful of Christian students as an example and leader of what it looked like to live for Jesus in a public high school.

Yet as the preacher boy, I had lamented the fact that I held the attention of not one girl. Now I suppose this wasn't quite true. But it sure felt like it was. Over the previous summer I had met this girl Nikki while volunteering at a Bible camp. Our affection was mutual, so later that summer I had driven a couple hours each way to take her to watch Will Smith save planet Earth in *Independence Day*. That was the first date I had ever been on. It was cool but just way too long distance to hold the practical side of my attention.

There were a few other girls that struck promising notes of interest. But they were also from camp, not high school, and the dichotomy between the two worlds could not have been bigger. At the one I was a leprous imp to be avoided at all costs. This was high school, and it was my reality. But at the other I had somehow acquired a mark of celebrity among the camp's junior-level staff that seemed to grow each time I returned. And it included an increasing number of friends, many of whom were girls wanting to hang out and take long midnight walks through the forest. Remember, though, we were devout Christians, so rather than making out, we spent those long midnight walks talking about spiritual mysteries and divine purposes.

The dichotomy drove me crazy. The few weeks of summer camp that I enjoyed each year became a fairytale world, an illusive existence held far, far away from me during the remainder of the year. Back home in "real life," my paltry list of friends felt humiliating. I continued to value my divine calling over any given social circle, but that doesn't mean all cravings of status evaporated from my psyche. And the feeling that Bible camp gave me of pseudo-popularity made my high school cravings all the more palatable.

But what I really wanted was a girlfriend. Or at least a date. *Something!* I just wanted to be able to look at a member of the opposite sex without receiving those torturous rolled eyes. Anyone from my own town who was just kind of good-looking would have made a worthy candidate, so long as they could have held it together without a gag reflex when making eye contact with me. But I seemed doomed nonetheless.

Until this one girl came along. She worked with me at the grocery store and went to a different high school. She was older and dressed with an edgy provocation. She was flirty and fun and fairly attractive with a fit body. This girl asked me to give her a ride home to her family's ostrich farm after work a few times. And she would make these dirty little jokes with me in the car. She asked me about my sexual history and offered to tell me all about her own. *Such a tease.* And the more we talked, the hotter she became.

But there was a problem. She wasn't a Christian. Shocking, I know. No evident faith and no church whatsoever. And being the disciplined and serious young man that I was, I refused to let her interest lead us anywhere. And the rides home had to stop. Lest I fall into temptation . . .

I began venting my romantic frustrations to some of those close to me, such as my youth pastor and a couple other students from the church youth group. I labored over my commitment to date only equally devout Christian girls and lamented the fact that there weren't any of those that I was interested in. None of the prettiest and most popular girls seemed that interested in the things of Christ. And if any girl was remotely interested, either she lived thousands of miles away—*such as my missionary crush who worked at church camp and lived in Guatemala*—or she just wasn't someone I was that attracted to. But if push came to shove, I was a hormone-riddled sixteen-year-old, and I was seriously rethinking my commitment to date only devoutly committed Christians.

The responses I received from all my confidants were united. God understood my frustrations, but he was also bigger than them. All things were in his control, and he would provide when the time was right. Every single person emphasized God's pleasure that I took my faith so seriously. And every one of them promised that God wanted to bless me greatly in return. I was assured that at just the right time God would reward me with an unbelievable woman of incredible faith.

And now we come to the prayer.

You know, the third of *the three.*

See, there was this amazing girl in my grade. Her name was Justina. Undoubtedly among the circle of most popular females in our class, she was universally recognized by the male student body as the hottest girl in school. A couple years later in our yearbook's Senior Hall of Fame she would be elected two honors: "Class Flirt" and "Most Secretly Desired for a Date." And as for me, I had *secretly desired* her since she moved to our small town in the sixth grade. She always mocked me as "alien head," but never mind that. She was drop-dead gorgeous, and I rarely took an eye off her for the five years that followed.

The prayer spontaneously arose within me as I was standing in the hallway one afternoon late that fall. Like all weird teenage boys who also happen to lack any romantic experience, I just stood in the hall for a few minutes that day, just blatantly staring, watching Justina at her locker. Just standing there, soaking up every move she made. Kinda creepy, but in a Jesus-loving sort of way . . .

And that's when I prayed. In a brief moment of divine address, sincere yet kind of lighthearted, I remarked to God, "You know, Lord, if it's true . . . If you really do want to bless me for my faithfulness when it comes to girls . . . I cannot think of a greater blessing than Justina. God, I pray that you would make Justina come to faith in Jesus . . . Yeah, God, please make Justina a Christian so that we can date and get married. Give her faith in Jesus and then give her to me as my wife . . . God, what a blessing that would be!"

I can't say that I really thought he would do it. Some who believe in "signs and wonders," some of the "name it and claim it" variety, argue that God wants to grant all of our even most materialistic prayers, but that such prayers require *faith*. When we pray for a new car and don't receive it, it is likely because we didn't truly *believe*. Anyway, I didn't really believe God would give me Justina. But it was sort of a fun prayer to just toss up to the lap of my Heavenly Father, letting him know that it sure would bring me delight to see him take such an interest.

And he did. Granted, God also gave me some strategic insight along the way. By that strategic insight, I invited her to youth group. And since Justina had shared on occasion about how much she'd loved attending an eighth-grade retreat to Bible camp, I invited her to join us for that year's upcoming fall retreat as well. Everywhere I went, I looked to find her and would then strategically place myself around her.

And wouldn't you know it, she decided that yes, indeed, she would like to join us on that retreat. Unfortunately, however, she came down with a resurgence of mono and had to leave the retreat early. But even here, I took the opportunity to call and check on her a few days later. This was, of course, back before texting and cell phones were a thing. So we could only make actual phone calls while sitting inside enclosed houses back then, but her illness provided me a justifiable excuse to do so.

And that call led to other calls. And over the weeks that followed, I found more and more reasons to call her as we found more and more things to talk about. And then one night over the phone, I shared one of those evangelistic talks I had learned about at the DC super-conference a couple years earlier. She was going through a lot at the time, and all my God-talk triggered within her an overwhelming flow of emotion. And that night she prayed "the prayer" to ask forgiveness of her sins and to accept Jesus as her Savior and Lord. Just a couple months from my hallway prayer, Justina was now a True Christian.

But that answered only half my prayer. She still had that boyfriend.

But that boyfriend was two years older than her. He partied a lot and was less than the best influence on a young girl who had just committed the rest of her life to following the model and teachings of Christ. So it made sense that over the next few weeks she felt increasingly uneasy about her relationship with this boyfriend of hers. And as our phone conversations grew more frequent, she apparently grew more and more attracted to me.

Then on New Year's Eve, December 31, 1996, Justina broke up with her boyfriend at 5:30 p.m. and showed up at my door at 7:00. Felt pretty *badass*— though I wouldn't have used such profanity to describe the feeling back then. It was our first date. And it ended with a kiss on the cheek. Like the best of '80s comedy, the dork got the girl in the end.

Prayer 75 percent complete.

We married June 24, 2000. Justina was my second date, my first girlfriend. We even "saved ourselves" for the wedding night. And three and a half years after that first kiss, we became husband and wife. We did everything by the book, a perfect picture of an ideal courtship in the mind of any evangelical Christian.

We even stopped along the way to attend the DC '97 super-conference together. Justina was the girl of my dreams, and they were all coming true. Clearly, God had answered my relationship prayer as a sign of big things to come.

Questions for the Dialogue

Our story has thus far focused on the circumstances of three transformational prayers. Let's discuss.

For Everyone

- Whether you personally believe in the power of prayer or not, how would you go about determining whether something happened as the result of prayer or the result of some other mix of conditions or circumstances? Is it possible to verify answered prayer scientifically?

For Believing Christians

- What are some of the most powerful answers to prayer that you've experienced? How did they impact your own faith?

- Have you ever been convinced that your prayer had been answered only to discover later that it really hadn't been?

- Do the prayers of this story look authentic and genuinely offered to God in faith? If so, how so? If not, why not?

For Atheists and Skeptics

- Have you ever experienced powerful events that you once attributed to supernatural origins? How do you now explain them?

- If you had grown up in an environment where powerful events were regularly attributed to God, how might it have influenced your views toward faith?

- Many Christians feel justified in their beliefs due to a long list of personal experiences. Is it appropriate for believers to view answered prayer as a level of experiential observation on par with scientific observation? If not, is it understandable to see how some might view it this way nonetheless? How so?

Chapter Three

Burning Zeal:
When Faith Consumes the Teenage Life

I had a recurring vision. One that continued reprising itself throughout my last year of high school. It wasn't necessarily a glimpse of the *future* per se. Nor did I ever attribute it to *supernatural* origins. And I wouldn't quite put it on par with the Book of Revelation's magnitude.

But it was just as terrifying.

While walking through the hallways to my next class, I would suddenly see all my classmates burst into flame. Or I would be working my cashier job at the grocery store, when all my coworkers and all the shoppers would abruptly catch fire. Or while driving down the street, a small blaze would ignite inside every passing car.

At least a couple times a week for months on end, I witnessed this unseen event take place over and over and over again. And regardless of location, the details I envisioned were the same. Everyone around me continued on their way, having no idea they were on fire. But they were. Their entire beings consumed by the flames of hell, and they had no idea. Even more terrifying to me, however, was the reality that I saw myself just standing there as I watched them burn. I watched myself do nothing. My complacency allowed me to stand idle as they all burned to the ground completely unaware.

Another variation of my vision involved a swimming pool. If I knew my loved ones were drowning in the backyard, would I simply take mental note only to then return to life's more comfortable activities—or would I run out there and jump in the water and save their lives?

Be it the flames of hell or the waters of the world's cesspool, these visions brought an inner conviction against me. I was far more complacent than I had had any right to be. Against the explosive resound of a biblical call to action, I was dallying on the playground of piss-poor excuses and lackadaisical daydreaming. But I couldn't stand by idle anymore. It was my job to rescue. *How could I just stand there silent as those around me lost their lives to Satan?* I had to do something. I had to say something. God had called me to stand up and intervene. He had called me to do more. A world of death needed the Good News of salvation. And I would answer the call.

And so even before I started envisioning flames and pools, my entire high school experience was consumed by the pursuit of ministry. Not that all other interests were sapped away by religion, I still had quite an interest in girls as discussed earlier. And I enjoyed art—albeit, it was often religious art. And I also loved movies. *Seriously, I watched a lot of movies . . .* But nonetheless what got me up in the morning and what put me to bed at night was the desire to do more and attain more and *be* more as a representative of Jesus Christ on this earth. And given the fact that I was a student, my mission field was my public high school.

Horribly uncoordinated in my athletic experiments, even less abled in my musical attempts, and often feeling as if my only friend was Jesus, I gave an accumulating share of my time and attention to things of faith. After that sixth-grade prayer that rescued me from the throes of suicide, my entire social calendar increasingly revolved around my youth group's weekly gatherings and fellowship events. And by high school, my constant presence had made me a dependable staple member. So along with my artistic abilities, I also began volunteering my fearlessness before an audience and my eagerness to lend a hand wherever it was useful. Assisting in service projects and fundraisers, teaching lessons to the congregation's younger children, and otherwise serving as a dutiful attendant of all things church, I did it all. I was there for it all. I genuinely *enjoyed* it all.

Meanwhile, our church's youth pastor was a guy named Pastor Jeff. He was a late twenty-something single, and like me, he too seemed to have few friends. And so the two of us ended up hanging out a lot, watching movies or engaging in deep late-night conversations. I would meander across town and up to Jeff's office a few times a week after school, and we would spend many Friday nights hanging out. We'd just sit in his office for hours on end discussing theology and philosophy and movies and girls and whatever. Sometimes my other friend Bruce would join us, but usually not. Sometimes I felt like I could speak more openly and easily with Pastor Jeff than I could with anyone else in my entire life. And sometimes I would think that that openness was pretty incredible considering our fifteen-year age difference. But all this in turn opened the invitation for me to focus even further on ministry and church in my all-consuming passion for Jesus.

And so church and Jesus and faith and ministry truly did become my everything. And the more active I grew, the more admiration I began to receive from the church's adults. I became the teenager that every senior citizen doted upon. Even the church's senior pastor and leadership began recognizing me more and more. And honestly I *relished* the attention. And the more involved I became in religious activities outside our little church, the more veneration I received from our entire town's religiously inclined citizenry.

Though I had already latched onto an upfront role in my church's junior high youth group, I took things to a new level in my ninth-grade year of high school. Then fresh from the heights of the DC conference, I was eager to form a new and more public stage for my faith.

That year, I started a weekly Bible study after school. We met in a cleared-out upstairs hallway, or sometimes in the stairwell. We never sought permission to move to a classroom. I didn't want a classroom. That would be too private. Obviously we could have studied in a church building somewhere, but we wanted to invite God's work *into* our school. I wanted to declare this *his* territory. And as such, part of the gathering's purpose was to bring our biblical and theological discussion within earshot of passersby.

Not that we wanted to be loud and obnoxious. Our study was genuine and not a staged show. We weren't following a script, nor were we merely pretending to study. Our activity was real and honest as we read and discussed God's work in our lives. But at the same time I wondered if God might plant a spoken word or verbalized Bible text into the heart of someone as they passed by in the hallway. So there we placed ourselves, and no one ever asked us to move. Teachers either ignored or encouraged us, but no staff or faculty member ever challenged or questioned us. So in the hallways and stairwells we remained. And there we sharpened and encouraged one another. There we grew in our faith as followers of Jesus.

The study was never very large, but we met weekly for three and a half years. Its membership cut across the denominational lines of several churches, though

I found it challenging to move others toward what you might call an *active* participation. I would have everyone in the group take turns reading text and verbalizing prayers, but when it came down to selecting the topics of study or the particular texts themselves, everyone regularly looked to me with a stubborn reluctance to do or say too much. I suppose I really can't say I was too greatly bothered by this, since I really did enjoy playing group leader. And if you caught me in a confessional right now, I might also profess to have been a bit of a control freak.

The Bible study led to other ministry opportunities as well. Our group took part in other larger activities, such as the "See You at the Pole" event, where students of faith gather around the flagpoles of their local public schools to pray for the nation and its teens. And I was invited by faculty members on a couple occasions to pray with them or help them make sense of any particular Bible verse.

In my tenth-grade year I took the weekly Bible studies a step further and began monthly worship services that took place before school. For this I did have to get permission, allowing me to book the band room for our meeting place. I was surprised to find that the worship services appealed to a different mix of kids. Those classical musicians who had no use for Bible study nonetheless enjoyed an additional outlet for their art. And some of the regulars of afternoon study had no interest in getting up for an extra-early school day. As a result, this morning service proved to have its own unique presence in our school.

All of this was off the school's books. No yearbook photos or recognition as an official extracurricular group. No faculty oversight—none were ever present at anything I led. But I loved the grassroots feel of it all. I often felt it was just me and God, slowly enveloping our entire school with the Spirit of Christ.

As teens of faith talked more and more about the excitement of our activities, I believed a true movement of the Spirit was on our hands. So like with any quality movement, I figured we needed a newsletter of course. I laugh about the idea now, but I took it very seriously back then. *Yes, we definitely needed a newsletter.* It would serve as a great vehicle to gain awareness to our activities while also generating cross-denominational unity around the work we were doing. And as an added plus, I kind of liked the challenge posed by the further responsibility.

I decided to collect all my various efforts under the banner "God in Our Schools." And so the only logical name for the movement's newsletter had to be *The God in Our Schools Newsletter.* Mind you, our efforts focused only on a single high school in one lonely district. But the plurality of the movement's title was intentional since I had already been taking steps to expand our efforts to the other schools of our district and dreaming dreams of expansion to surrounding towns.

Six times a year I composed my little two-page newsletter, chronicling our latest advancements and outlining our future endeavors as we worked to flood the school system with as much of God as possible. Every eight weeks or so, I would drive my car through town to all the churches and tack the newsletter up on foyer bulletin boards. I included all nine churches. Some questioned my decision to include the Lutherans and Methodists. And I was criticized a number of times for sharing my newsletter with the local Roman Catholic parish. But even then I was idealistic enough to believe that God could overcome the differences of creed and catechism. God was on the move, and we were all following wherever his Spirit should lead.

Because of all of this, the Minnesota division of the Baptist General Conference granted me the 1997 Christian Service Award based on the work I did for "God in Our Schools." From what I was told, I was the first teenager ever so recognized. Though there was no public ceremony, Pastor Jeff, who had nominated me for the award, presented me with a beautiful plaque passed along from the church conference's headquarters.

As "God in Our Schools" was building, my participation in our church continued growing as well. When our congregation needed a new senior pastor in 1997, I was asked to join the pastoral search committee alongside four adults. I then preached my first sermon on a Sunday morning in the spring of 1998, exhorting the entire church to get more serious about spreading the gospel and saving souls. You can also add to all this my annual summer work on staff at our church conference's Bible camp up on Trout Lake and my stint as a floor counselor when the good reverend Billy Graham came to the Minneapolis Metrodome back in 1996.

But hold on here.

The purpose to writing all of this is not to parade my spiritual superiority or innovative wonder, but simply to show that, be it for good reasons or for bad, this is what my entire teenage life revolved around. I lived and breathed ministry. It was all that ultimately mattered. And I really believed in it. I was in love with God. He was all that mattered and all I really needed.

When driving in my car, I would hear love songs on the local pop-rock radio station, and in my mind I would envision singing them to God. He was the higher romance of my heart, the Only One that really mattered. Not that I was planning a life of celibacy. Justina was my girlfriend through much of this, and I took our romantic love seriously. But I recognized our love as functioning on a lower plain beneath the ultimate love-relationship I enjoyed with God, the Lover of my Soul. One time, I even chided this new girlfriend Justina for giving me a Valentine's

Day card that claimed she treasured me "above all else." How blasphemous, I told her. God alone is to have primacy in our lives. So no, I'm not using these pages to attempt a parade of my spirituality, but rather to demonstrate the all-consuming nature of my faith from an early age.

But full disclosure: In all my activities, it was also great to feel like I was actually good at something, like I had a role to play. My life had a purpose. And I was living out that purpose in school and in the Kingdom of God. I was called, gifted, and empowered. I filled a need for that which others seemed inadequate. And honestly it provided an alternate narrative for me to shape my loneliness around. I was no longer unpopular and friendless because I was worthless; I was those things because I was willing to give up such worldly allures for the sake of Jesus.

I assured myself and others around me that I *could* have had all those other "worldly" things but that I had chosen a higher path instead. I was something along the lines of a martyr. That's how I saw myself. Ignoring all the social challenges I faced, I reshaped the story within my own soul and convinced myself that I could have lived the stereotypical teenage experience. But I chose to sacrifice it for the Kingdom. I chose Jesus as my only friend. He was all I needed. And I would work tirelessly on his behalf. I would martyr my days in service to my Lord.

Questions for the Dialogue

Let's open this up a bit to consider the various means and motivations of anyone entering religious service.

For Everyone

- How do the events of this chapter correspond with your own personal experiences? Can you imagine any teenage circumstances where you might have undergone similar actions?

- Had it not been for this teenager's religious convictions, how might his high school experience have been different? What elements of the story here, if any, might seem like a normal part of being a teenager? Of the story's more eccentric parts, what's your impression of them? Are they commendable or concerning? How so and to what degree?

For Believing Christians

- Do you think it's possible for someone to have a sincere and genuine desire to serve God even if they also desire the attention they receive in return? Or does the latter invalidate the former? If so, why?

- What does it look like to be fully committed to one's faith? What does the transition from less faithful to more faithful look like? Is it possible to have perfect faith?

- What kinds of motivations are acceptable for one who wants to become a pastor or other religious leader? What kinds are unacceptable? How often do you think it might be a mix of motivations?

For Atheists and Skeptics

- Under what circumstances might it make sense for a nonbeliever to enter religious service? Are there any? If so, what?

- Take a moment to consider, do you see anything constructive from the events of this chapter? Any good that could come from any of this teenager's actions?

- How do you think the social component affects the draw of most people toward religion and even religious service? Have you experienced a strong sense of nonreligious community? How has it affected your own response toward religion?

Chapter Four

On Mission:
Building a Life of Purpose and Passion

Alright. So now that the foundations of my all-consuming faith are in place, this is where I build it into a life and career—the part of the journey that spanned from zealously fundamentalist teenage preacher to progressive-but-ever-believing-and-hope-filled pastor. Of course, everyone's story is different. We're all walking this earth on our unique path, but we're also walking our paths together. Thus, much of what follows may seem foreign to some, while it may seem familiar to others.

Given my developing reputation as a teenage almost-preacher, our church's senior pastor approached me with college advice when I was in tenth grade. Pastor Jeff was my youth pastor friend, but this was Pastor Wills. Pastor Wills was kind of a jolly guy with a big laugh, but he also had this intensity that always made me wonder if he wasn't at least a little pissed off. And in stark contrast to my super-close friendship with Pastor Jeff, Pastor Wills was shrouded in this mystique that I found both crazy intimidating and yet wildly intriguing all at the same time. Pastor Wills had just earned his doctorate and was going to be leaving our small-town church to go someplace larger that could probably pay him a better salary.

I guess Pastor Wills knew I was thinking about pursuing some form of professional youth ministry, and he asked if I had ever heard of the Moody Bible Institute before, located far away in the Big City of Chicago. I hadn't, but he told me that it was one of the most well-known and well-respected Bible colleges in the world, that they specialized in ministry preparation, and that due to its amazing reputation, donations from across the globe regularly flooded the school, covering 100 percent of all undergraduate tuition.

He described how Moody created a garden oasis right in the middle of a dark and thirsty city. He really said that. *A garden oasis in the middle of the dark and thirsty city.*

I imagined blocks and blocks of cloudy grey skies stacked with burnt-out cars and rapists. And right there in the center of it all was this opening in the atmosphere with the great glow of heaven streaming down upon a ten-acre campus of towering trees and singing birds, all clapping for joy in the name of Jesus.

But Pastor Wills also said the application process was rigorous and featured a two-year waiting list. If I was at all interested, I had better apply ASAP.

It turned out the waiting list was a widespread yet bogus rumor that the school routinely worked to dismantle. But I didn't want to take any chances, so I applied right away and they held my application on file for two years.

My small town's small church took great delight in sending me off to the faraway land of Chicago to study at the place where Christian legends are made. Moody was a serious place. One of the seven admission essays I had to write explained how I knew for sure that God was "calling me into Christian ministry." I also had to declare a major upon application. I selected to study toward a Bachelor of Arts in Youth Ministry, though all the old ladies in our church said they knew God *really* wanted to make me a great preacher.

Meanwhile, my grandfather—the real homespun fundamentalist in our relations—shared his fears that in going off to study theology at *any* institution I would inevitably fill my head with a bunch of liberal nonsense about the Bible. He had heard of far too many men who had started off as great pastors but then got one too many degrees and strayed from the faith. He implored me to not let any liberal nonsense I might learn at Moody corrupt the purity of my belief. But I told him that if God was in me, he could surely harness any acquired knowledge to strengthen my trust in him, that I had no reason to fear its deterioration. And then I marched forward.

I had never thought too critically about the Bible prior to college. I mean, I had read it a lot. In other words, I carefully walked through a couple chapters each morning and prayed over them with devotion. But I had never worked too hard to make much *sense* of it. Not that I didn't try. I'd read and reread the verse or paragraph or chapter until it *at least kind of* made sense, but if anything seemed particularly confusing or illogical or even offensive, I'd just set it aside. I'd assume that that's what we had trained pastors and theologians for. I'd assume it made sense to them, that that's why we had them. But I wasn't one of them, at least not yet, so of course some of this stuff didn't make sense to me. *How could it?*

So I just did what most all of us do in evangelical churches. I kept my head down theologically and simply did the best I could to live out what I believed to be instructed. Since God's Holy Spirit was living within me and since I worked daily to submit myself to his leadership, I trusted he would direct my life and thoughts accordingly, guiding me as he saw fit to make any needed changes in understanding or in the application of such. If God wanted me to think differently, he'd change my thoughts. If he wanted me to live differently, he'd impress upon me that I should do so. And when he did, I'd follow dutifully. So there was really no need to worry about it. And I didn't worry about it.

Preaching and teaching at my hometown church were usually kept to a certain surface level of comfort. I remember one of Pastor Wills' Sunday sermons where he admitted to an inner wrestling over a particular theological issue. After years of consideration, he had finally concluded that the Bible did indeed teach the Doctrine of Eternal Security, another standard Calvinist tenet akin to Perseverance of the Saints that is pretty much a given in the minds of many evangelical churches. It insists that once a true Christian is saved from sin and hell and an eternity of God's wrath, she or he will always be saved and that their salvation can never be undone. Pastor Wills was saying that though this was a staple doctrine throughout much of evangelical Christianity, he had often struggled to accept it. And now he was saying that he had finally come to see its teaching reflected in the Bible. And then he explained why. But getting into all these theological details seemed unusual to me. Normally our lessons were a bit more simple and focused on the practical application of stories and principles.

So until Bible college I had never even heard of Calvinism or Arminianism, or of Dispensationalism or Covenant Theology. I had never heard of Chrysostom or Augustine or Zwingli, and certainly not Jonathan Edwards. But it all started streaming in during that first year at Moody.

Prior to Bible college, the only Martin Luther I had known of was the Reverend Martin Luther King Jr. And I often wondered what he did to start the whole line of churches named after him. But I didn't look into it too intensely. A couple of family members had warned me that Martin Luther King Jr. was a liberal fanatic used more of Satan than by God. So I kept myself in line and steered my faith hard to the right.

In truth, for how serious I was about high school *ministry*, I really wasn't much of a scholar on any level at all. I did just enough to get by in my studies and that's it. I mean, the only two books I had read prior to college other than the Bible were *To Kill a Mockingbird* and that John Grisham book with Tom Cruise on the cover.

There was almost a third. In the eleventh grade I had started reading *The Grapes of Wrath* in my junior-year literature class. But I was so offended by its characterization of the fallen preacher and its use of curse words that I refused to read further and wrote my English teacher Mr. Palmer a letter of protest. He and I had a special meeting in the library to discuss, and I think he had a hard time trying to figure out what the hell was going on inside my head. In fact he came right out and told me, "I'm having a hard time understanding just what the hell's going on inside your head." So I willingly accepted a failing grade on the paper. Because I was a martyr.

So I entered Bible college knowing I wasn't a serious student. But I also knew I would now be studying the Bible and really sincerely wanted to become a serious student. I couldn't have cared less about high-school studies, but I couldn't have cared *more* about the boundless opportunities to really truly honestly engage the world of Bible-college-studies.

And I knew I would be doing lots of reading. So I did what anyone who has barely read three books in his entire life would do. I did the only logical thing you could do if you wanted to be a serious student but also knew you weren't one. I read a book about reading books. I searched Amazon and ordered Mortimer Adler's *How to Read a Book: The Classic Guide to Intelligent Reading*. I took care to apply its principles and suggestions. And to this day I honestly think of Adler every time I pick up a new book.

So yes, the most amazing part of Bible college was acquiring the practice and joy of reading and studying and critically thinking. I loved it. I really did. And the more I read and studied, the more I wanted to read more and study more. I longed to marinate my mind in every phrase and fragment. I was a slow reader, mind you. But almost every academic discipline I encountered was an exhilarating first exposure. I opened my mind and ran wildly through the vast fields of thought and inquiry.

This is probably why I had little interest in college play. I joined in on an occasional dormitory prank or weekend excursion, but mostly my life was about devouring every concept I could. I needed to make up for lost time, catch up on all the theological jargon that so many of the other students seemed to be born into. I quickly realized that many of the others had grown up attending churches where they talked regularly about Calvin and Edwards and where they had heard of the Doctrine of Eternal Security much earlier than I had. But that wasn't a problem for me. I would just determine to work harder and study longer and eventually pass them by. Whatever must be done in service to my King.

My grandfather the homespun fundamentalist maintained a large voice in my life and psyche. And he always charged me to stick with the Bible alone. "The Holy Spirit is in you," he would admonish me. "Don't believe anything just because someone tells you to. Only believe it if you can see it with your own eyes written in the Word of God." This principle was built deeply within my soul. It taught me to question everyone and everything. And to never believe or do something just because an authority tells you to. But most importantly, his regular admonition freed me up to eagerly go wherever I saw the Bible going.

During my freshmen year, I even encountered a bit of a theological crisis as I had a hard time seeing where the Doctrine of the Trinity came from. I couldn't see it in the Bible just yet, and if it wasn't in the Bible but was some subsequent theological innovation, I knew I needed to part with it. I was seriously considering leaving mainstream Christianity for a version of modalism or maybe some other nontrinitarian variation of God. But I knew that if I made such a move I would be forever declared a heretic, damned by virtually every segment of Christianity. So I felt led through prayer to trust the conclusions of the historical church and keep the Trinity. At least for now. I figured even in my extensive six months of Bible training there were probably things I just hadn't understood quite yet. Things that would come later. *Don't become a heretic just yet,* I convinced myself. And yes, it was true. Through the years, I would eventually come to see the Trinity in the Bible, and it would then bring me great joy to help connect those biblical dots for others to see.

But all this to say, I never believed anything just because my professors told me to. I questioned it all. Building on the mentality my grandfather gave me, Moody developed in me the critical tools needed to use against every other stream of theology, that is, against anything that wasn't Calvinist or Dispensational in leaning. And I used those tools eagerly. I questioned every book, every lecture, every postulation. The larger concepts I mostly adopted as my own, but I felt free to modify and alter what didn't sit right with me. The brand of Classic Dispensationalism articulated by most Moody profs seemed to me just a bit too ideological, restrictive, and rigid. I didn't stream too far from home base, but I found more freedom and flexibility in *Progressive* Dispensationalism, and this is the camp I would play within throughout my pastoral ministry. But the Calvinism I ate up. The more I studied, the more it seemed to make sense of the Bible's teachings, and I would grow to ardently defend and support it, at times crafting new phrases to help bring fresh understanding to those around me.

But Moody also showed me an active side to the Christian faith. I had gained the impression growing up that faith was merely a "personal relationship with God" and that morality was limited to individual disciplines, such as those regarding sex and substance abuse. Any religious work that attempted to help those in financial need or contribute positively to society was relegated to the world of a *social* gospel, which was also a *false* gospel. But at Moody we were shown that true faith was always active. It played a role in the world around us and served humanity with compassion and grace.

One of the school's hallmarks was the distinctive value it assigned to tangible Christian service, assigning each student a weekly duty for the semester. This was called the student's Practical Christian Ministry or PCM.

Apparently, so the legend goes, Dwight Lyman Moody, the great traveling evangelist who founded the school, insisted back in the early days that only the morning would be given to academic instruction, reserving every afternoon for going out to do hands-on ministry around the city. *An inactive faith is no faith at all*, we can hear the spirit of old DL calling us today. *Who needs a bunch of head knowledge that fails to change the world*, he continues to beckon.

And so I spent every Wednesday afternoon during that first semester working with a group of junior high boys at an inner-city community center that was placed along the dividing line of two rival gangs. Another semester I spent my Thursday evenings visiting with senior citizens at a nursing home for those with mental disabilities. Though some PCMs were geared around teaching the Bible or sharing the Good News with passersby, other ministries were more tangible. Simply representing Jesus as a servant to humanity, loving people unconditionally on his behalf. No script. No overt evangelistic agenda.

One thing that Moody excelled at in my own spiritual development was in training me to maintain this active approach to faith, not one contained in an ivory tower of academia. I had previously understood *ministry* to be activity that was reserved for Christian pastors and leaders alone, but in Bible college I came to realize that this was the very nature of faith itself, that God expected such work of *all* his followers. Moody both deepened and expanded what I understood to be the active side of faith. If our belief didn't drive us to bandage wounds, feed the hungry, and clean up after the sick, and if it failed to propel us to *go to* the masses needing to hear the gospel, then whatever faith we held to, it wasn't Christian, not truly. To claim Jesus as ours we actually had to *live* like him.

The summer following my sophomore year, I started an internship at a local Chicago church that would quickly turn into a part-time position on pastoral staff. By this time, I had switched my major to Pastoral Studies after realizing I wanted to work with the whole church rather than just its younger segment. And I had come to this midsize Evangelical Free Church congregation and its five hundred members because of its strong reputation as a training ground for biblically minded pastors. My time at Bethel Community Church would last seven years, and here I found a great opportunity to put my growing passions and theology to work.

I served as pastoral assistant, working alongside the church's senior pastor in virtually every facet of church ministry. Visiting the sick and counseling the troubled, leading Bible studies and teaching classes, attending staff meetings and planning worship services. Soon I was preaching on Sunday mornings and launching new ministry initiatives. I took a couple years to design and launch a new coffeehouse ministry that served as a gathering place for those in the neighborhood to come and connect, providing opportunity for those from our church to get to know them and simply be a voice of compassion and love in their lives. I then trained up a team to take over the coffeehouse, so I could shift my focus to something new.

I loved a good challenge. And at the sprightly age of twenty-five, pastoring a group of some seventy-five senior adults seemed like my next great adventure. "Senior adults" is code for *old people*, and given the huge age gap between myself and them, especially given their propensity to complain about all of Bethel's ongoing changes, this indeed seemed like a great opportunity for my next big ministerial hurdle. But I didn't mind their inclination toward criticizing innovation. In fact, as part of my love for a good challenge, the devious side of me almost *enjoyed* confrontation. So I would relish any occasion when one of the seniors would be griping and complaining and "causing trouble" over a new change in how the church did things.

I would be sent in to meet with whichever senior was upset about the drums being too loud or a new programing decision. On occasion, if it was a widespread concern, I'd call an open meeting with the entire group. My adrenaline would be all supped up at what was often a daunting task to calm and enlighten a group of concerned or even furious grandparents. Adrenaline would run high, but I couldn't let it show.

I would enter such meetings with a firm gentleness and speak with compassion. I would lay out the biblical arguments supporting the changes and attempt to clearly articulate our goals and thought processes on the issues involved. I would speak in love. And I would confess that though none of us on staff were perfect and though we surely made mistakes along the way, all our decisions were nonetheless made in a prayerful attempt to honestly serve Jesus and his people as best we knew how. And I was often humbled by their receptive and encouraging response. By the end of the meeting, we were almost always united in hugs and prayers. They didn't *want* to be difficult. But they too were just trying to serve Jesus as best they knew how.

I grew to love them, and they seemed to clearly love me. They cared deeply for my growing family and adored my two young daughters. Though I was in graduate school by then and working full time at a downtown steakhouse to pay the bills, I was able to etch out a couple days a week for those seniors, and it truly became a labor of love as I devoted three full years to their service. They came to me with their concerns about family and church, and we prayed and read the Bible together. We had two Bible studies every week and went on monthly outings as a group, just having fun and experiencing life with one another. And eventually, for some of them, I officiated their funerals and shed real tears over their caskets.

As my time at Bethel was winding down, so was my time in seminary. I had followed in the degree of choice among young ministers by obtaining what's called a Master of Divinity, a three-year professional degree that's kind of like an MBA for ministry practitioners. Though years back I had hoped to attend seminary at another institution, finances compelled me to remain at Moody for my master's as well. Though Moody Graduate School (or MGS, currently known as Moody Theological Seminary) wasn't quite tuition-free like undergrad was, I stretched my master's from three years into six and managed to pay the whole thing off as I went along, eventually graduating debt free.

And I found a renewed love and academic vigor in seminary. Though Moody undergrad had grown stale and predictable in its conservatism and tradition, MGS retained the same conservative theology while engaging a much more progressive methodology. We were always pushed to think outside the proverbial box in how we applied God's Word to life and faith. We were set free and emboldened to experiment, to take risks and never fear mistakes. God was in control and he had called us to tread new ground and accomplish greater works in his name. My eyes were opened and heart racing as I saw God providing new challenges and empowering me to craft new solutions. I felt like I was on the edge of a new world.

And even in seminary, much of Moody's emphasis was on the practical. Ministry excursions included work to raise community awareness toward Chicago's growing epidemic of human trafficking. And during "emersion nights" in an LGBT neighborhood we refrained from any preaching but simply came to sit, listen, and learn about abuses done in the name of Christ. We were being trained to approach with humility and empathy while also thinking critically about how to initiate steps of reversal within the church, taking a posture of grace and compassion to the world around us, rather than one of judgment and condemnation. MGS was all about compassion and embrace in Jesus' name. I loved every moment of it and in turn would lead groups from my churches on similar projects.

As I was nearing the end of seminary, I was also preparing to transition out of my position at Bethel Church in search of a full-time spot elsewhere. And as classes were wrapping up, I met with one of my professors. He had become something of a mentor to me over the years, and I pretty much treasured everything he said as rare gold. Seriously, I idolized this guy above any other. But that afternoon he attempted to steer me away from pastoral ministry. He told me that I might very well make a fine pastor one day but that what he really saw in me was the heart of a true scholar. He could tell I was a deep thinker, a fearless critic of tradition and assumption, and that I produced solid and thorough academic work. He had another seminary all picked out for my PhD and was prepared to write me a recommendation right there on the spot. He was confident I could likely get a fully paid fellowship with stipend, if I were only willing.

The only problem: I wasn't. I told him that I appreciated his affirmation and attention—and all the guidance he had provided me over the years. I even admitted that a return to academia might sound appealing in the future. But not now, definitely not now. I was all too eager to exit the academic life and finally clear my full schedule for hands-on ministry. No more time wasted on writing papers I didn't want to write or reading books I didn't want to read. No more paying bills by waiting on tables. I just wanted to get out and be active. I wanted to lead and accomplish and build God's kingdom.

And those days brought another opportunity across my path as well. It's here where I was first offered a management position at that downtown steakhouse. My bosses seemed more than a little perplexed the first time I said no. But after I turned it down a third time, once again reminding the general manager that I was a pastor and was planning to leave the company by the end of the year, he looked at me with a sly grin on his face and said, "So church work must bring in pretty good money, huh?"

I laughed. *No, the money was actually pretty terrible*, I replied.

He laughed even louder.

"Well, then what the hell's the problem? Let's make this happen!"

But I wasn't in it for the money. *Money*, I told him, *was the last thing I was looking for*. I simply wanted to serve God and his church. That's it. And I told him so. Ministry was my single and unshakable passion. Everything I had ever encountered over the course of my entire life had brought me to this moment, and nothing would deter me now. Not the full ride of a PhD and certainly not a six-figure salary. I wanted more of God and of his people, and that's all that mattered. Nothing else would get in my way.

In July of 2008, I was offered a position as pastor of a small struggling church in the Chicago suburb of Westmont, Illinois. Always eager for a challenge, I went to West Hills Community Church to attempt a "turnaround" that would bring revitalization by making whatever changes necessary. The church was named West Hills because it straddled the boundary between the villages of Westmont and Clarendon Hills. It was located on the highest point of all DuPage County. And it was to be a community of Jesus' followers who bridged groups and united humanity. But it had suffered a long line of recent staff crises, devastating a church of 350 people and shrinking it down to just 32 in less than three years' time. But upon taking a closer look, I believed God could still bring healing to this withering community and was willing to help lead the way.

Much of my work, of course, focused on the regular responsibilities of preaching and teaching, Sunday worship preparation and study, board meetings and counseling sessions, program development and staff oversight, and weddings and funerals. And in many ways my time at the church was delightful. Though I suppose it's true that I'd always been a bit of a workaholic and that it's not always easy to remain relaxed when one is voluntarily out of balance, I nonetheless found the work incredibly rewarding. It was exactly what I had looked forward to doing full time for so many years.

I found few thrills as exciting as experimentation with new ministry practices. And here at West Hills, they allowed me the playground to attempt "doing church" a little differently than what most of us were used to. I pushed envelopes and searched for new approaches. We kept it fresh and lively. And through it all, the church members pitched in with rolled sleeves and enthusiastic smiles.

I was trained in seminary to expect a one-year "honeymoon period," after which the church would start focusing on my faults and I on theirs. They would realize how flawed I was as their pastor and a section of the church would begin to define themselves with opposition. But in my four years at West Hills, this never happened. They were always loving, generous, and abounding with patience.

Every one of them. They were ever eager to consider my perspective. And they let me lead. Even those who weren't always on board with every decision I made were nonetheless gracious enough to keep disagreements private and maintain a good relationship with me. Likewise was the congregation's love and enduring hospitality for my family. The depth of their embrace was unexpected and has forever marked me. I will always be thankful for my four years with them.

But I was there for a purpose. It was to redesign the congregation into a thriving organization that grew with vitality and strength. We slimmed down and redeveloped the ministry structure, placing an emphasis on fostering a true and loving biblical community. This community of faith was to be a vessel of love and compassion to the world around us. To embody a true and genuine transformation that extended beyond our own campus.

And within that world around us, our church worked to recreate itself as a positive and constructive presence within the surrounding community. In the spring of 2009, we launched the Hands Projects Initiative. Our small church of fifty people partnered with others in the community to "put our hands together" in practical acts of service to our neighbors, seeking to represent the loving servanthood of Jesus himself. Our projects were varied: cleaning up a local park; girding up the foundation of a local widow's house; serving refreshments to the community after a 9/11 commemoration. One time, we undertook a landscaping project for a nonreligious organization that housed medically fragile children.

And each November we organized our largest event of the year, where we packaged and gave away Thanksgiving dinners to those in the community who otherwise wouldn't have one. By the third year we were giving away feasts with full-size turkeys to 350 families, feeding well over a thousand people. We invited others in the community to partner with us as we served together in the name of Jesus. There was no sermon. No religious tracts. No prepackaged attempt to proselytize. They already knew we were a church, and if they wanted theological information, they could ask. We simply wanted our community to know first and foremost that we were there to extend a helping hand and love them without condition.

In 2009 I was also ordained. Though Christianity's many variations approach the subject quite differently, in the Baptist tradition, ordination is the process whereby a believer is recognized and affirmed as having been called by God into vocational Christian ministry. It also serves as an endorsement to the individual's doctrinal positions and methodology. A fully distinct process from one's seminary education, this is a rite that can only be done by the local church, but advisory boards are called upon to help examine candidates and provide recommendations.

Though I had been doing ministry now for well over a decade and had previously been called upon to help evaluate other candidates, I had waited to seek my own ordination until seminary was out of the way in 2008.

All this to say, at the age of twenty-nine and now in my first full-time pastorate, I reasoned it was time to go before our church conference's advisory council. Baptist churches reject the idea of the top-down hierarchy normally characteristic of denominations and instead cluster themselves into networks of likeminded churches, which are called *conferences*. West Hills was part of the same Baptist conference I had been a part of in my small-town Minnesota church, but the organization had since changed its name from the Baptist General Conference to Converge Worldwide.

This is because the word "Baptist" had increasingly acquired a negative connotation in American culture, which in turn had led more than 50 percent of the Baptist conference's Baptist churches to take the word *Baptist* out of their names. In response, the Baptist General Conference followed suit and changed its name to Converge Worldwide. It decided to keep BGC as its legal name while designating Converge Worldwide as its *missional name*. This was because names like Converge were shown to do a better job reaching new people for Jesus than those with "offensive" words like Baptist.

When I went before the group of fellow Baptist pastors that made up Converge MidAmerica's ordination advisory council, I was told that my succinct fifteen-page doctrinal statement was the most well-written they had seen—though with a bit of a snicker, some of them might have also mocked my dispensational theology as naïve and distinctive of a Moody education. The council said that they usually asked young guys like me to wait a couple years before being entrusted with the weighty credentials of ordination, but that since I seemed to have a strong head on my shoulders, they'd grant me express lane access to gaining their recommendation. West Hills Church then took their advice and acted accordingly.

Throughout my time at West Hills, my labor of love was preaching and teaching the Bible. I have never experienced anything as exciting and invigorating as standing before hundreds of people—*or even just fifty of them*—to proclaim the Word of God. There's just something spiritually electrifying about it. As with many pastors, the Sunday sermon simultaneously supplied both thrill and frustration. It's not easy crafting a brand new 45-minute monologue each week along with the many other demands of organizational leadership and pastoral care. Seminary had taught me that a well-researched and seriously crafted sermon required ten to twenty hours of preparation time, but I was able to manage it in something more like seven or nine hours for most workweeks. Early on, I learned to balance this with the frustrating realization that even the greatest sermon would only be delivered once before being discarded for another. At times I felt like a sermon-machine, just pumping them out one after another, week after week. But I nonetheless loved it. It was in my soul and had become a part of me.

In many ways, though, what I loved even more than Sunday sermons was in-depth small-group Bible study. I loved the interactive discussion. We sought to create a safe space where participants could apply their own perspective to the text, believing that the Holy Spirit could use any of us to teach truth to the rest of the group. But invariably, they looked to the pastor to provide most of the insight and direction. And I really did love answering their questions. It was hard to beat the pulsating rush of not knowing what would be asked next and then needing to think quick on my feet to construct and present the appropriate answer. And since most of our study time was devoted to open discussion, I would prepare answers in advance for any related topic that was less familiar to me. Walking into our 90-minute Bible study sessions, my brain surged in anticipation of how God would shape our time together.

Then a few times each year I would hold "Ask the Pastor" sessions where, instead of focusing on a specific chapter of the Bible or a particular theological concern, I welcomed any and every question pertaining to the Bible or the spiritual life. I would be asked about random topics and concerns and whip up answers on the fly, putting my biblical understanding and theological perspective to the test. Members of other churches who normally didn't attend our weekly study began hearing about these times together and would come to join us.

Sometimes I felt like a theological gladiator. Stepping into the room with dry-erase marker in hand, adrenaline churning as I took up my Bible in this extreme sport of the soul, I would teach for hours on end and never want to finish. Sometimes we would bring study to an official conclusion so people could leave if need be. But the rest of us would stay and study further as I flooded the front wall with timelines and diagrams.

The reason for my excitement really came down to empowering people with greater understanding. I was a pedagogical junkie. Always searching for new methods to bring clarity and new phrases or illustrations to stretch perspectives, I was addicted to seeing those *Aha!* contortions of the face. I thrived on helping others approach faith in new and fresh ways and equipping them to find greater understanding in the process.

Ultimately, though, I just wanted to challenge believers to take their faith more seriously. I wanted to equip them for following Jesus more vibrantly. I wanted to flood my people with the joy of a relentless discipleship that was in complete surrender to the Spirit of God. I saw these goals manifesting themselves in ways I never expected as my teaching took root and began to spread powerfully throughout our church and in the surrounding community. It was amazing. And it was humbling to be allowed such a leading role.

But it was also haunting.

For underneath the surface, I recognized a growing gloom. And it was becoming impossible to overlook. Even as my faith propelled me out further and further into new ministry opportunities and adventures, even as I began writing a book on discipleship that was a far different book than this one, a looming darkness was gathering. A mounting storm was already seizing upon my robust and indestructible faith. And sure enough, the winds of a tornado were about to tear through, dismantle, and obliterate it.

Only a couple years into my arrival at West Hills Church, another story began unearthing itself in my heart and mind. Even as I thrived on sharing and articulating my faith, it was silently cracking and crumbling from within. I could save others, but I couldn't save myself.

And this is the story to which we now turn.

Questions for the Dialogue

Much has happened in this chapter, and there is much that could potentially be discussed. Let's see if we can pick up on some of the larger discussion topics.

For Everyone

- When you envision a faithful and believing evangelical pastor (or other religious leader) what do you see? How does the pastor in this story compare?

- When you envision the kind of pastor who would eventually quit believing in God, what do you envision? Again, how does the pastor in this story compare?

- What kind of person would devote their entire education and career to religious service? What might such actions say about such a person? How likely is it that someone would do so under false pretenses? What would be the potential risks and rewards of doing so deceptively?

- How does knowing that this pastor would eventually stop believing in God influence your assumptions about the faith of other currently believing pastors? How does it influence your assumptions about the faith of currently believing laypeople?

For Believing Christians

- Returning to an earlier discussion topic, do you see any reason to question the sincerity of this pastor's motivation? How does his motivation toward the practice of his faith seem to compare with your own?

- Do you see any indications that this pastor's faith might not be genuine? How does his belief in God compare with your own? Does it seem more fragile than your own faith, or is it about the same or even stronger?

- If you knew nothing about the rest of this pastor's story, is there anything here that would make you suspect he was about to walk away from his faith and ministry? Do you find it surprising that he would? What's your reaction to learning this?

For Atheists and Skeptics

- Sometimes it can be easy for skeptics to assume that Christian pastors don't actually believe what they say they do, that they're in it for the power or the fame or maybe even for the money. How do these ideas square with your own preconceptions of a religious leader? How do these ideas square with that of the story found here in this chapter? Does this pastor seem genuine? Does it seem he really did believe it all? Does it seem he really was coming from a position of good intentions?

- Do you see anything here that would make this pastor more or less likely to eventually stop believing in God?

PART TWO:
THE EVOLUTION OF DOUBT

Chapter Five

Questions:
The Stubborn Little Desk Drawer That Could

The beginning of this second story really gets started back before there even was a second story. It begins with the simple process of study and research and the asking of questions and finding of answers and the asking of more questions and finding of more answers. And of then asking some questions that return less-than-satisfying answers that lead to more questions with *eventually* satisfying or *at-least-kinda*-satisfying answers. We're reminded of psychologist Jerome Kagan's work in uncertainty resolution and of Arie Kruglanski's work on the need for closure. Yet we're also reminded of times and situations in our personal lives where the available answers still failed to fully satisfy. And so we held onto those answers lightly and tentatively even as curious eyes remained on watch for something more—something *better*. And all in a grand pursuit to understand this world that we live within—and to understand what it *means* to live within it. This is the basic process we each use—*quietly and in the background without notice*—to learn and to discover, as the beings of humanity that we are.

Now, along the way, we've come up with various tools to help us in our pursuit of knowledge. These tools are often kind of sciency and stuff, but one of the newer ones is so basic that many of us take it for granted every single day. We might even laugh when we hear its name. It's called Google Search. And Google Search allows us to locate answers to a wide variety of questions fairly easily.

Last week, for instance, I was given a recipe that included something called *mirepoix*. I had no idea what mirepoix was, and I'm guessing I'm not the only one. Microsoft apparently doesn't know what mirepoix is either, since it keeps underlining the word with a red squiggle mark every time I type it.

Back in the antiquity of the 1980s and early '90s, my options would have been pretty limited in the grand pursuit to understand and discover the meaning of mirepoix. Those options would be to travel to the local grocery store and ask one of the workers there if they knew what mirepoix was or to knock on all the doors of my block asking all the little old ladies if they knew what mirepoix was or to pick up a bricklike thing connected via curlicue cord to a telephone box on my wall and use it to call the downtown culinary institute and inquire of a master chef. But let's be honest, most likely I would have quickly quit caring what the hell mirepoix was and I'd have returned to jumping up 8-bit flagpoles in my grand quest to rescue the peachy princess from the depths of a mushroom kingdom.

But this isn't 1987. And now we have magic phones that have been liberated from wall boxes. So instead I just picked up my phone and within about five and a half seconds, Google told me that mirepoix was "a mixture of sautéed chopped vegetables used in various sauces," where "the traditional ratio is two parts onions, one part carrots, and one part celery."

So much easier.

And I've long since stopped rescuing 8-bit princesses because I'm having so damn much fun learning and discovering the meaning that Google assigns to new words.

But the point is: When we have questions, we're used to looking for answers.

Now sometimes—*and this is important*—the answers don't feel satisfying. Maybe they don't appear believable or are from a source that seems to lack credibility or maybe they just prompt a negative emotion and we begin a grief cycle of pretending it couldn't be true even though we kind of already know that it really is.

Often times, when our questions return answers that aren't satisfying, we set those answers aside and keep looking for other possible answers.

This is normal.

We all do this.

And so my pre-second-story-beginning stretches all the way back to the simple practice of setting information aside. Just as this is a common practice for the entirety of an inquisitive humanity, so it is also a common practice for evangelicals who are trying to find a specific set of answers to everyday questions that also squares nicely and comfortably with what they already believe to be found as true within their Bible. We'll talk more about the evangelical commitment to the

Bible's flawlessness in the next chapter, but for now we're simply pointing out that for the evangelical mind, the pursuit of understanding must coincide with one's understanding of biblical teaching.

This is true of all evangelicals. And so it is true of evangelical *pastors* as well.

I like to talk about something I call my *little desk drawer*. It's not a literal or physical desk drawer, mind you, but one that exists in my mind and possibly even in all of our minds. Others have drawn upon similar concepts using a variety of imagery to portray the same basic idea. It was British minister Leslie Weatherhead who in his 1965 landmark *The Christian Agnostic* extended to skeptical believers the freedom to file away difficult-to-swallow doctrines in what he calls a *mental box* marked "Awaiting Further Light." And former pastor John Compere also speaks of an internal drawer in his book *Towards the Light*, a drawer that had eventually grown "filled to the brim" with unanswered questions during his own process of deconversion.

It's not difficult to envision how such a drawer and its desk might function. The mind's *desktop* is reserved for those matters deemed most pressing for the moment, projects currently being dealt with. It's for those concerns, both theological and other, for which we feel more properly equipped to handle. And there on that desktop of the mind we address them confidently. We entertain questions and engage in conversations. We think through implications and pass them along to others.

But then once in a while we come across other discoveries, be they mere opinions or robust data sets, which are not so easily dealt with. They serve to challenge our previously held answers and readymade conclusions. We attempt to tag and file them within our neat little system, but then we realize we're not quite sure how to fit them in. And the more we look at them and think through them, the more we realize how ill-equipped we are to properly process them, at least without having to seriously rethink the entire system.

For the evangelical, we're talking about challenges regarding the flawlessness of the Bible or the comfortability of our theology. It could be the archeological studies suggesting that the cities of Jericho and Nazareth were destroyed long before they show up in biblical timelines. Or the historical records suggesting the wholesale invention of characters such as Darius the Mede and an earlier rendition of Governor Quirinius. Or maybe the fossil records that challenge the underpinnings of the Bible's teachings on human origins.

Now when your desktop's confidently built on the assumption of a flawless

Bible and then something comes along to challenge the validity of such a foundation, I suppose you do have a few options. But most likely you begin by doing a little digging of your own. You assume the challenge is flawed and that its flaws will grow quickly apparent. And you're sure the challenges *must* be flawed due to your great confidence. After all, this almost *has* to be the case since your entire framework is built on the truth of an error-proof Bible.

But then sometimes, as you dig, the evidence seems to point more and more strongly toward the validity of the opposing critique. *So what do you do?* Now some may more easily cast aside their commitment to an errorless Bible, but for many evangelicals this takes a different direction. Instead, they simply stop the search. Or at least set it on pause. As my friend Leslie explained, such critiques often find themselves in a box labeled "Awaiting Further Light."

The thinking is that eventually more information will come along, and when it does, the Bible will certainly be vindicated. So in an act of trust, the challenge and all its concerns are placed to the side, to the periphery. Figuratively out of sight and out of mind.

In that bottom right-hand desk drawer.

And this plays out with a fair amount of predictability:

You're doing a little research, and the evidence raises questions about the validity of Darius the Mede? No problem, just slide that paragraph into your mind's bottom right-hand desk drawer.

You're watching the History Channel, and it explains that the Bible has two completely independent creation accounts blended together with irreconcilable differences? No problem, just slip it in that desk drawer.

While perusing the latest issue of Time *magazine, you're reminded once again of the ongoing findings brought to us by the work of evolutionary science?* Not a biggie. That's why your mind has a desk drawer. Just pull that handle and toss the whole damn article inside. Enjoy a deep breath of relief as you hear the drawer slamming closed behind it.

Out of sight.

Out of mind.

Well, until . . .

Until the day you open your drawer to slip yet another item of critique inside, only to find the unthinkable happens. It was unthinkable because you had grown accustomed to not having to think too much about what's down there. But then. Then one day you open the drawer and begin to conveniently file away something from your afternoon reading, only to discover your convenient little desk drawer now refuses to close. The drawer is stuck.

You look down to see what the problem is. Only to discover that so much stuff has been accumulating in that little desk drawer that the drawer itself is jammed open even as its contents now begin to overflow.

And you can no longer keep them to the periphery.

The drawer is stuck open and its mess is simply too large to ignore—it now demands your attention. *How can one return to the work of the desktop when an overflowing drawer threatens to overturn the entire desk itself?* And so it's at this point that you are forced to finally pull out all that little drawer's contents. You pull them all out and spread them across your desktop. *And it's here* where you finally begin to deal with it all.

This was my experience.

This was my desk drawer.

In the next chapter we're going to examine the kinds of things that fill such desk drawers of the evangelical mind. But it's going to be much more of an introductory tour than an exhaustive analysis. It's more like if you come to visit me in The Fine City of Chicago. I'd love to take you on one of our wonderful architectural tour cruises. They're three-hours long and escort you all up and down the Chicago River and along the lakeshore. They're marvelous and amazing and expose you to much of what I love about my home. But honestly, they can only provide the highlights. A quick intro for tourists. The only way to *really* know Chicago comes from years of driving up and down all the side streets and walking each of the neighborhoods, from eventually leaving the skyscrapers of the Loop and the exciting nightlife of River North. Only then do you ever really begin to perceive the details of the fuller picture.

Same here. Detailing the many—*many*—layers of information that had been filed away in the desk drawer of this evangelical pastor's mind could fill a book of its own. This is especially true when considering the sheer volume of challenges posed against the Christian Bible from a broad spectrum of disciplines— archeology, biology, history, and so on—as well as theological concerns centered on the process of the Bible's origin and the fact that biblical prophecies that should have been fulfilled long ago just haven't been. Indeed, a lot of great books have already been written on these and other overwhelming challenges to the Christian hypothesis. Several are offered in this book's resources section, and you'd be doing yourself a favor to check them out.

But to provide an example of just one layer of the various challenges flooding the evangelical mind, we focus next on what may be the most foundational layer of all, detailing some of the Bible's own internal inconsistencies. I mean, seriously, when the Bible can't even be reconciled with *itself*, that's a pretty big deal. Maybe even the biggest deal. Which is why we shall now shift our attention to the challenges raised by the Bible's own words.

Questions for the Dialogue

Our questions here are simple. Let's dive right in.

For Everyone

- In this discussion about mental desk drawers, we've suggested that everyone— both naturalists and supernaturalists—more or less has one. Would you agree? Do you have one?

- What kinds of basic assumptions might shape the desktop of your mind?

- What are some critiques to your beliefs or perspectives that you're honestly not sure what to do with? What are some challenges that you've filed away in your own mental desk drawer awaiting further light?

Chapter Six

.·ıllı.·ıı·ıı·ıı

Cracks in the Wall:
Biblical Contradictions and the Work
of Reasonable Explanations

Forty-eight of fifty U.S. states are divided into what we call "counties." Such as Central Minnesota's Mille Lacs County, where I was born and raised. But Louisiana divides its county-like geopolitical regions into "parishes" instead. And Saint Mary Parish is just one of sixty-four, located right on the Gulf and in the heart of the bayou.

Now as you might expect, it's not always the easiest task to attract visitors to the heart of the bayou. Maybe it's the alligators. Maybe the humidity. But either way, in 2010 the Cajun Coast Visitors and Convention Bureau broke ground on a new $3.8 million convention center in an effort to attract more tourists. The new center was to feature exhibits on the parish's offshore oil and shrimping industries and would be designed around a Cajun-cabin theme, featuring local wildlife like alligators and black bears. The idea was to pull traffic through Saint Mary Parish in order to sell a tank of gas, a night at a local motel, anything to generate a little economic boost to the impoverished community. Local government invested the money. And Cajun Coast set to work.

Fast-forward two years. Here we find the story as it entered one of my final sermons, delivered in the days before my pastoral preaching drew to a close. In June 2012, two years into the convention center's construction and just three weeks prior to its scheduled grand opening, a local painter discovered a crack in one of the walls. And after getting another set of eyes on the minor concern, it began transforming into an even larger one, as this little crack started stretching its arms wide across the sheet rock. So they decided to evacuate the building for further inspection.

That's when the majority of the Cajun-themed convention center busted off and sank a full five feet into the swamp. As one observer noted, the whole thing "cracked like an egg."

Did I mention the center was built on a swamp?

Well, I apologize. But yes, it was indeed built right there on top of the watery muck. And knowingly so. Somehow the architects and engineers thought that certain soil samples gave them the go-ahead to build on it anyway.

I guess Saint Mary Parish had never heard of that famous parable. You know, the one that teaches how wise men build houses on the rock instead of on shifty surfaces like sand . . . and swamp.

Now, I wholeheartedly confess that I know nothing about engineering or architecture or soil samples. I really don't even know anything about swamps for that matter. But I have to wonder how much time members of the Cajun Coast spent wondering if building on a swamp would hurt them in the long run. I'm curious if they just took the info and quickly pushed it to the back of their minds—fingers crossed—in hopes that the inconvenient information would simply go away. *After all, if you close your eyes real tight, reality does bend to your wishes, does it not?* I wonder how many times, once the project broke ground, these guys woke up in the middle of the night fearing that the worst was about to happen.

But my point here is that it did. Reality did settle in. The facts could only be ignored for so long. And eventually two years and three million dollars later, the whole thing fell apart.

Eyes closed tight and fingers crossed can only go so far.

Eventually even our greatest beliefs can break open like an egg and sink five feet into the mud and muck of an inconvenient reality.

And so we now step into a sampling of the problems and issues that eventually pulled my faith toward collapse. And as we mentioned at the end of the previous chapter, we're doing so by focusing here on the Christian Bible itself. And on its ability to agree with itself—or, more accurately, its *lack* of ability to do so.

Now it's the goal of what theologians call *systematic theology* to make the Bible speak in one rational voice. It is to take all the disparate pieces of information and blend them together, to merge and to harmonize them into one another, to compliment biblical teaching with insights from philosophy and science, psychology and archaeology, in order to present an all inclusive understanding of everything there is to know about God and about the things of God. It is to account for all the data and make room for every tiny little detail. It is to create a theological *system*. The practice can be a little tricky at times, but it can also be really exciting to consider how all the pieces fit together in a Big Picture sort of way, at least for a nerd like me. I was one such nerd who found the work of systematic theology to be absolutely *mesmerizing*.

And so in one's reading of the Bible, if something doesn't quite fit—maybe it's hard to see how the séance with the Witch of Endor and her conjuring up Samuel the Prophet from the dead squares with everything else the Bible says about death and the afterlife—or maybe Jesus' teaching doesn't always sit well with us when he requires his followers to hate their families or curses the Canaanite people as dogs unworthy of his attention—if something in the Bible doesn't quite square at face value with the rational or comfortable, then it is the job of *systematics* to just keep spinning it in various directions until we find just the right angle to view it from, allowing it to ultimately fit more easily within the system.

And that practice of spinning and fitting, it works for most things in the Bible.

But not for everything.

It can be hard enough to harmonize the Bible's opposing theological statements. But the most difficult parts to bring together are those tiny details of hard data, such as conflicting census results from a certain year or the age of a particular king. If the Bible can't get this stuff right, then we have a serious challenge toward its accuracy and therefore its credibility. If the Bible contradicts with other historical records, the believer's task is simple: just declare the other sources as corrupted and keep your trust in the Bible as the only truly inerrant historical document. But when the Bible itself has two answers that are simply incompatible with one another on a hard-data level, *just what is a believer to do?*

So what we have for you here are ten examples of the Bible's many internal inconsistencies. Five from the Old Testament and five from the New. But rather than simply showing the problems and moving on, we want to demonstrate how diligently the evangelical mind works to dismiss them. In doing so, my hope is that evangelical laypersons will more clearly see the textual problems that are usually covered up without their notice and that all others will gain a clearer understanding as to why evangelicals continue to believe in the Bible's flawlessness even when its errors may seem so blatant to the rest of us.

As a pastor I was aware of each of the following examples but, as you will see, I worked to explain them away as best I could for years on end. And to the degree that my explanations still failed to fully satisfy, well, that's where my desk drawer came into play. I would push them to the side and keep them from focus, simply trusting that we must be missing something. But alas, one final contradiction would simply prove too grandiose for my abilities to sweep away, and it was one that ultimately, years down the line, would help push my faith in biblical credibility to its breaking point. Yes, we're gonna talk about this one as well, and yes, we're gonna save it for last.

When the Numbers Get Jumbled: Old Testament Confusion

Let's begin with this. We find King David and the army of Israel under wartime duress in Second Samuel 24. Life has not been easy for God's chosen nation nor for its king. And so we read that Israel's god Yahweh—*that's the name that much of the Old Testament uses to refer to the one Christians simply call "God" today*—Yahweh gets angry and "incites" David to number his northern and southern troops as they ready for battle. Maybe David was feeling a bit anxious at the moment, maybe it was pressure from his advisors, or maybe it was pure fear, but either way, in Second Samuel 24 David gives in to God's temptation and counts his warriors in order to estimate his ability to win.

But this is a problem. Though Yahweh himself was the one inciting the king to number his troops, he apparently considered it a major sin to actually do so. And once David gave in to that temptation, the wrath of an angry God would now cascade upon him. See, David's census proved that his ultimate trust was in the physical strength of his army rather than in his God's ability to provide victory regardless of the numbers. His faith was in humanity instead of in Yahweh. And for this breach of faith, David must be punished. For the crime of giving in to the prompting that God gave him to count his warriors, David must be reproved. He and his whole nation.

And so as the story goes, God approaches the prophet Gad to give King David a choice of punishments for his crime. The king gets to pick his sentence, and he has a choice of three options: (1) seven years of famine promised to cripple the entire nation; (2) three months of wartime defeat where his people will be continually on the run under the constant pursuit of stronger enemies; or (3) three days of horrifying plague that will obliterate a large portion of the population. Either way, Israel is going to suffer immensely. Each option is devastating.

And King David refuses to choose. I think possibly the most noble part of this whole story is the fact that the king stands firm in the face of his god and refuses to choose how his people will die. David has many faults, but he will not play games with the lives of his people.

Anyway, Yahweh is forced to make the choice for him, and over the next three days he uses a deadly plague to kill off seventy thousand Israelites. All because the king should have blindly trusted his god to hand him military victory without making practical preparations like counting troop levels. All because King David gave in to a temptation offered by the very god who judged him.

There may very well be several troubling—*even horrifying*—aspects to this story. But these are not our chief concern here. Questions about the character of true faith or about the nature of sinful actions or about the temptations of a holy god, these can all be explained away using one theological *system* or another. But there's, dare I say, a much *bigger* problem here.

The problem is this: the story is told twice.

The Bible repeats many of these stories from Israel's early days. First in the books of Samuel and Kings and then again later in the books of Chronicles. And this story from Second Samuel 24 is told once more in First Chronicles 21. But there's a problem in this second telling. One detail doesn't quite match up. And the difference is a little too glaring.

Now in case you're not too familiar with how evangelicals and other Christians regard the Bible's status as God's Word, we want to remind ourselves that it is considered flawless. *Inerrant* is the world that's usually used. Perfect error-free communication delivered from God himself. Each chapter and verse. Every single phrase and word. Given by God and guaranteed to be true in every sense.

Though historians commonly find discrepancies within other sources from antiquity, there is a difference here. We *expect* human sources to include a mistake here and there, because after all, humans make mistakes. And just because a human makes a mistake doesn't mean the whole of his or her claim is to be discarded. We use and refer to historical documents written by flawed human beings all the time. We don't throw the whole document away just because it has an error or two—or even if it has a couple hundred. We simply recognize its worth for what it is, approaching it as a nugget of history that has its own context within the story of humanity.

But if it is claimed that the Bible is *100 percent inerrant* and yet we find in its pages even a single error, then we have a problem. We may still find some sort of value listed there—maybe even incredible value—just as with any other historical document. After all, any religious holy book can serve as a tremendous resource, providing great historical insights into the lives of ancient communities—and yes, *even when mistakes are present.*

But if we find a single error among any of its pages, then one thing we know for sure is that this book can no longer be considered *inerrant*. It still contains historical value, yes, but as *inerrant* it can no longer be held. It rather becomes just another source of ancient human perspective. And all of its contents yield their assumed authority to the same scrutiny with which we hold all other books against.

Now back to King David. Instead of threatening him with *seven* years of famine, here in First Chronicles 21, Yahweh threatens him with only *three*. Maybe because God softens up a bit in this version or maybe just because it better parallels the three months of being pursued and the three days of pestilence. But either way it is changed.

And so we ask of the Flawless Word of God, *which is it?*

Three years of famine or seven?

Clearly there's a problem here. Now, the good news is that everyone sees that. Even the earliest readers of the Hebrew Bible saw it—*the "Hebrew" Bible is the holy book of the Jewish religion, featuring the same basic set of books as the Christian Old Testament but arranged differently and sometimes with different names.* And even they saw the discrepancy here, and when in the second century the Hebrew Bible was translated into the Greek Septuagint, the decision was made to change the famine of Second Samuel from *seven* years to *three*. This was done, of course, to harmonize Second Samuel 24 with its obvious parallel account. We know of the change through copies of ancient manuscripts that date from before that time. The earlier Hebrew Bible said *seven*, and then later the Geek Septuigent changed it to *three*.

But most English readers today wouldn't even be aware of this issue since the majority of contemporary English Bibles continue with the Septuagint's modification. So if you open your own copy of the Bible's New International Version or its English Standard Version or any of a host of others, you will see in Second Samuel 24:13 that God offered David *three* years of famine even though the actual Hebrew text of that very verse claims it was seven. Christians might be appalled to find that their Bible translators are making changes to the divine text. But at least the stories within their Bibles appear to agree with one another.

So much for trusting the inerrant Word of God . . .

And yet, when Christians first hear of contradictions such as the one above, the initial thought is usually to assume it's just a fluke of some sort. That this is an isolated event, and that maybe if we better understood all the details of the situation, we would realize that it really posed no problem at all to their Bible's credibility (*cue the desk drawer* . . .). But unfortunately, such an assumption couldn't be further from the truth.

And so to demonstrate, we want to look at yet another discrepancy between the stories of Samuel and Kings and those of Chronicles. Yet another contradiction. And as we see, the scenario repeats itself.

First Kings 4 documents the widespread wealth, power, and wisdom of King Solomon. It records the vast quantities of his flour and meal, of his oxen and sheep, of his land from Gaza to the Euphrates. And within the list of King Solomon's possessions, an accounting is also made of his horse stalls—40,000 of them under Solomon's oversight. Or at least, that's how First Kings records them.

But in Second Chronicles 9 we find another accounting of Solomon's possessions. Not only is the record placed at the same chronological point of this king's story, but every detail is also nearly identical. However, when we come to Solomon's horse stalls, we see they are only counted to just 4,000 rather than 40,000. Just 10 percent of the earlier amount, almost as if God accidentally forgot a zero.

Honestly, 40,000 stalls is a bit excessive, is it not???

And here too, just as with the previous famine example, the Septuagint caught the error and changed the First Kings amount from 40,000 to 4,000. And here too, a good many English Bibles follow suit. You will likely read of only 4,000 horse stalls in your own Bible. And the number in First Kings 4 will indeed match that of Second Chronicles 9. But even though it matches in the version of the Bible that you hold in your hands, it only takes a little digging to see that we have *not one single Hebrew manuscript collected from throughout the whole of history* to support what's placed in front of you. Most Bible translations will note these changes in footnotes while attempting to explain away the fact that they have attempted to improve the very document they also claim to have been divinely inspired and inerrant.

Like I said earlier, it only takes one error to evidence the whole collection for what it is.

But the Bible doesn't keep track of ages any better than that of plagues and horse stalls. Let's begin with King Ahaziah and the age at which he was enthroned. Second Kings 8 makes him king at the age of twenty-two while Second Chronicles 22 makes him wait until he's forty-two. *So which was it?* Again, translations do the work for us and harmonize the two contradictory figures. They decide twenty-two is more likely, and doctor up your own Bible to present a smooth copy of God's Word that won't trouble your faith.

But, oh, there's more!

Like the year of King Baasha's death. According to First Kings 16, he died in the twenty-sixth year of King Asa's reign. But Second Chronicles 16 claims that Baasha lasted an additional decade, finally laid to rest in the thirty-sixth year of Asa's reign. *So which was it? And how do we decide which part of God's Word is more inspired than the other?*

One more quick example: Second Kings 24 testifies that Jehoiachin became king at the age of eighteen, and this is the age Bible harmonizers tend to deem the most originally inerrant. However, Second Chronicles 36 is under the impression that the sitting king was still a boy, enthroned at just eight years old. Eight or eighteen? A teenage monarch or a child-king, which do we go with?

And have you noticed yet how many of these variants are simply off by a digit?

This is just the Old Testament. And these are only some of the most glaring examples. There are more, many more. But honestly, even if this is all we had, even if there were only five contradictions in the entire Bible, isn't this enough? Isn't this enough to prove that the entire package, though possibly a great and valuable ancient resource, is nonetheless a simple *human* resource? And clearly not so supernaturally flawless in its credibility rating?

And yet, did you also notice that every one of these examples comes from the same part of the Bible? Each contradiction arises when comparing the four books of Samuel and Kings with the two books of Chronicles, two sets of documents describing the same portion of Israel's alleged timeline. When the Bible records one event twice, botched "facts" are readily apparent. Unfortunately most of the Bible records an event only one time, thus giving its readers no choice but to accept that single recording at face value. But wonder for just a moment how many more contradictions we'd have if the whole story was told twice. It would surely make for redundant reading, but it would also make it more difficult for believers to dismiss the painful reality: the Bible is flawed.

Lest we cave to the temptation to think this is just an *Old Testament problem*, let's pivot to the New, shall we?

New Yet Unimproved: New Testament Contradictions

The very first chapter of the New Testament's very first book gets us started rather well. The Gospel of Matthew begins by revealing the Savior Jesus' family tree in an effort to connect his lineage with the Davidic throne as a fulfillment of Old Testament prophecy.

The very first verse tells us plainly that the whole point of the provided genealogy is to evidence that Jesus was, in fact, the long-awaited Christ and the descendant of both King David and Father Abraham. And it does indeed argue that Jesus' paternal bloodline stretches all the way back, extending through Joseph, David, and Zerubbabel all the way to Abraham himself. *All good.* Not quite sure how this bears upon the chapter's *second* half, where it insists that Jesus was born of Mary, a virgin, who conceived by the power of God's Holy Spirit, and thus *adopted* by this human father named Joseph. Not quite sure how the bloodline of his *adoptive* father proves anything about his own, but we'll leave that to the spin of the theologians. We want to stick with the hard data.

And here's where we find another of those rare Bible moments where information is conveyed twice. Jesus' genealogy is also featured in the Gospel of Luke. But here in Luke 3, the family tree extends all the way back to the very first human, "Adam, the son of God." So, of course, we have some extra names in there, those linking beyond Abraham all the way to Adam. This makes for a longer list of names, but that's not a problem. Luke's genealogy simply begins earlier in time. And once Matthew joins in, the first chunk of names fall right in agreement, all the way up through David.

But that's where everything begins to fall apart.

That's where it all turns to chaos.

But before I say much more, let us consider the two genealogies (see table 1).

Of the information offered by our two genealogies, there are no discrepancies leading up to King David. But from David to Joseph, the contradictions leap forth like frogs on fireworks. Between David and Jesus, Luke's genealogy includes an additional fifteen names, forty instead of twenty-five. But to make things worse, of that list of names, only two of them actually match. Only Shealtiel and Zerubbabel are found in both. None of Luke's additional thirty-eight names appear in Matthew's list. None of Matthew's thirteen appear in Luke. They can't even agree on the name of Joseph's father.

Is it Jacob or Heli?

For this reason, some evangelical scholars, such as D. S. Huffman, have felt forced to conclude that only one of these genealogies actually claims to be of Joseph and that the other has to be of, well . . . *someone else?* They have to conclude that these aren't even the same Shealtiel-Zerubbabel combos and that this cannot be the same Zerubbabel of the biblical book of Ezra. Maybe one of the genealogies is talking about the famous father-son duo, but it can't be both or biblical credibility is feared to be in danger.

But the problem is hard to miss if you're looking at the data honestly: Matthew and Luke provide completely different records of Jesus' paternal grandfather. They

Table 1. Differences in the Paternal Genealogy of Jesus

The Gospel of Luke's genealogy reaches further back than the Gospel of Matthew's does. It includes twenty additional names, neither confirmed nor contradicted by the latter. Those names are: Adam, Seth, Enos, Cainan, Mahalaleel, Jared, Enoch, Methuselah, Lamech, Noah, Shem, Arphaxad, Cainan, Shelah, Eber, Peleg, Reu, Serug, Nahor, Terah. The table begins with the next name in Luke's genealogy and the earliest one in Matthew's, that is, with Abraham.

Gospel of Matthew, Chapter 1	Gospel of Luke, Chapter 3
Abraham	Abraham
Isaac	Isaac
Jacob	Jacob
Judah	Judah
Perez	Perez
Hezron	Hezron
Ram	Ram
Amminadab	Amminadab
Nahshon	Nahshon
Salmon	Salmon
Boaz	Boaz
Obed	Obed
Jesse	Jesse
David	David
Solomon	Nathan
Rehoboam	Mattatha
Abijah	Menna
Asaph	Melea
Jehoshaphat	Eliakim
Joram	Jonam
Uzziah	Josheph
Jotham	Judah
Ahaz	Simeon
Hezekiah	Levi
Manasseh	Matthat

Gospel of Matthew, Chapter 1 (continued)	Gospel of Luke, Chapter 3 (continued)
Amos	Jorim
Josiah	Eliezer
Jechoniah	Joshua
	Er
	Elmadam
	Cosam
	Addi
	Melchi
	Neri
Shealtiel	Shealtiel
Zerubbabel	Zerubbabel
Abiud	Rhesa
Eliakim	Joanan
Azor	Joda
Zadok	Josech
Achim	Semein
Eliud	Mattathias
Eleazar	Maath
Matthan	Naggai
Jacob	Esli
	Nahum
	Amos
	Mattathias
	Joseph
	Jannai
	Melchi
	Levi
	Matthat
	Heli
Joseph	Joseph
Jesus	Jesus

clearly claim to be tracing Jesus' lineage through the same guy, but they can't even agree on Granddad's name.

But though this rather obvious observation may seem hard to deny, there *are* ways, mind you. Entire hypothetical scenarios are dreamed up in an effort to show that it is *at least possible* to make both lists true and accurate, and to therefore justify spinning them as *inerrant*. Stories are made up that one of the genealogies is intended to be Mary's. This hypothetical nightmare is presented to evangelical congregations as if it's found in the biblical text itself. It *sounds* satisfactory and also ties in Jesus' actual bloodline. Everyone takes a deep breath as evangelicals once again defeat critical attacks against the Word of God. But such hypotheses are completely made up—*even more fictional than the actual genealogy itself!* There is nothing to support such conclusions other than one's own predetermination that the Bible *must be* inerrant. But the real truth is this: the Bible presents us with two completely contradictory versions of Jesus' paternal family history. And in so doing, it becomes clear: the Bible doesn't even know who Jesus' grandfather is.

So that's the first of our New Testament contradictions.

And just as with the Old Testament, clear examples of internal contradictions within the New begin stacking up rather quickly. They're stacking up so quickly, in fact, we're gonna give you a quick intro to each of them before delving in more fully. But seriously, it can be difficult to even put a number on the unending questions that seem to lurk behind the details of each account.

For instance, did Jesus' most famous sermon, the one from Matthew 5–7 and from Luke 6, the one that began with the Beatitudes and ended with the story of the wise man who built his house on the rock—the sermon that also included such injunctions as the need to love one's enemies, to hold back judgments, and to stay silent regarding the sawdust in your brother's eye—take place on a mountaintop or on a level plain? And was Jesus sitting or standing during delivery? The gospels of Matthew and Luke can't seem to agree here either.

Here's another example. When Jesus hung on the cross, did the soldiers place on him the scarlet robe of Matthew 27 or the purple one from John 19? And as long as we're reading what the Bible has to say about Jesus' crucifixion, what does it claim that his last words were? The gospels bearing the names of Matthew, Luke, and John each record those cherished final words, yet none of them seem to agree on what those words actually were. Was it according to Matthew 27:46–50?

And about the ninth hour Jesus cried out with a loud voice, saying, "Eli, Eli, lema sabachthani?" that is, "My God, my God, why have you forsaken me?". . . And Jesus cried out again with a loud voice and yielded up his spirit.

Or did it happen as Luke 23:46 describes?

Then Jesus, calling out with a loud voice, said, "Father, into your hands I commit my spirit!" And having said this he breathed his last.

Or maybe Jesus kept it simple, as John 19:30 claims?

"It is finished," and he bowed his head and gave up his spirit.

Maybe one of these narratives got it right. Or maybe not. But the one thing that seems clear is that they can't all be perfectly correct.

But saving the best for last, we have one final contradiction for your review. When we get to the death of Jesus' betrayer Judas Iscariot, we find two very different renderings. Matthew 27 has Judas plagued with guilt, throwing to the temple floor the pieces of silver he received from the chief priests for giving up Jesus, before running out to then hang himself under a cloud of self-pity and remorse. Meanwhile, the chief priests realize they can't keep the blood money, instead using it to secretly purchase a field.

But then there's another version of the story, presented in the first chapter of the book of Acts. Here Judas uses the silver to purchase the field himself but somehow mysteriously falls headfirst to the ground where his midsection bursts open and his intestinal organs spill out. The Bible's two renderings of this story are so opposite, their unity seems absolutely preposterous. So here too, we ask: *Which is it? How are we to decide what* really *happened??*

Preparing a Response: Defending Inerrancy

Evangelicals take seriously the call to know their Bibles inside and out. And foundational to this call is the banner exhortation of the book of Second Timothy. "Do your best to present yourself to God as one approved," it commands, "a worker who has no need to be ashamed, rightly handling the word of truth" (2:15). Knowing your Bible, that is, properly understanding and applying the Word of Truth, is seen to garner God's approval. The flood of fundamentalist Bible studies, Sunday school classes, and children's Vacation Bible Schools are fueled by the desire to know and "rightly" handle the Bible's countless words, phrases, and verses. The King James Version even connects this idea with that of literally *studying* the scriptures, translating it as a command to "study to shew thyself approved." And in so doing, King James himself earned this verse a customary spot engraved on Bible college and seminary walls all across the Western world.

It would be a tempting assumption to think that evangelicals are taught to not think so hard about the Bible, to put it away and simply trust in what their pastors and preachers have to say. But this is not necessarily true. Though some churches certainly have a bit more of that than others, many self-designated "Bible-believing churches" place a heavy emphasis on individual mastery of biblical contents. Their congregants are urged by leadership to know their Bibles well, to personally read and study and memorize, to dig into even the less popular corners of God's Word. And along the way, many evangelical pastors even exhort their people to think about biblical content from different angles and to imagine how reading it in its original context could help indicate the author's original intent, therefore providing higher-quality interpretation.

And oftentimes, evangelical ministers are well aware of their own potential for imperfect understanding, making it all the more important that their people likewise study independently. To guard against sermon calendars that are filled with personal preference and easy subject matter, many pastors force themselves to preach beginning-to-end and chapter-by-chapter—*even verse-by-verse*—through the entire Bible, just to make sure they don't inadvertently skip the teachings that are tricky, confusing, or potentially offensive. And a regular exhortation found on the lips of many such ministers is that their congregations be "as the Bereans of Acts 17." This is a reference to the Jewish Christians of the book of Acts who fact-checked the Apostle Paul's claims by "examining the Scriptures daily to see if these things were so" (Acts 17:11). *So know your Bibles and know them well*, many of today's Christians are told. *And be wary of the cult leader or heretic who distorts the Bible's teachings to fit his own agenda.*

But here's the key.

This exhortation carries with it an implicit assessment about the Bible itself. You see, the whole point of knowing it is precisely because it is held up as that divinely inspired and inerrant collection of Holy Scripture that we described earlier. And this command to "know your Bibles and know them well" demands that you study under the conviction that whatever it says, it has to be flawless and therefore authoritative. But if one dares step outside the fence of biblical inerrancy, it is automatically seen as a fail.

Inerrancy, you see, is the litmus test.

And the unwritten rule of evangelicalism is that inerrancy must never be challenged. To even consider the possibility that the Bible might not be *the supernaturally inspired, flawless, and completely authoritative Word of God* is to automatically push yourself outside the bounds of evangelical Christianity itself. So study the Bible, yes, but only within the boundaries of inerrancy. And should your study call its credibility into question, you have clearly gone too far. You have failed the task. You have transgressed the true faith. You have queried the one question that must never be queried. And in so doing, you have proven that you most certainly have *not* studied to show thyself approved.

We pause for such an explanation as this because it provides a glimpse as to why Christians feel the need to defend the Bible's credibility at all cost. Since evangelicals strive to live out the Bible as if it is a message from God himself, they have to be able to assure themselves that it actually *is* God's Word. And they have to be able to rise to the critique of anyone who challenges their assessments.

As an evangelical you can question just about any other theological tenet and push biblical application in entirely nontraditional directions. Your methodology may rigorously attempt to think outside old-school boxes. You may bend biblical words and meanings. You may spin contexts and design your own personal ideological grid. You can embrace all these things. That's all fine and even encouraged in some circles. But the one thing you cannot do, the one thing that is completely off-limits, that which diametrically fails the test of true faith, is to even consider questioning the legitimacy of the Bible's own literal word-for-word perfection. For fear that once this is done, once the Bible's own credibility is lost, the whole faith falls apart. The only reason we believe in God, so it seems from the evangelical perspective, is because the Bible tells us to.

And so, without fail, evangelicals will rise to the challenge.

Defend the Bible, they must.

Rising to the Challenge: The Evangelical Response

For starters, when it comes to the conflicting numbers of the Old Testament narratives, evangelical scholars will remind us that nowhere on Earth do we have a single original autograph of even a single verse of the entire Bible.

Umm, yeah, did you realize that?

Let me state that once more.

We

Do

Not

Have

Anywhere

on

Earth

a

Single

Verse

of

the

Original

Bible.

Just in case you didn't realize . . .

And so when it comes to those conflicting Old Testament numbers, we are simply reminded of this truth. You'd think they'd want to hide the fact that we don't actually have an original Bible, but there are times when such facts can be used to play to their favor. And this is such a case, I guess.

So it is proposed that in the original Bible—the one that none of us have ever seen—those two accounts didn't actually contradict one another. See, since the Bible is inerrant, obviously they couldn't have contradicted originally. And it is decided that a scribe must have made a mistake when copying the Bible. And it is further argued that every copy of the Bible we've ever discovered must have been copied from the one with the wrong number in it. So then we go back and reconstruct what we imagine the original flawless Bible must have originally said. We print our English Bibles with the correction and put a scholarly sounding footnote at the bottom to justify the "editorial decision."

And now there you go, we have just preserved the Bible's credibility. The "original autographs" were inerrant and flawless. We know because we can feel it in our hearts. God's Word must be true. Even though every copy of it that we've ever had holds contradictions. Never mind the fact that we've just made up what the Bible "actually" says in order to make it sound more to our liking. And just try not to think too hard about why God wouldn't just give us an original to look at. Push those questions to the side for another day, for a day that will never come.

But when we consider those New Testament contradictions sampled earlier, the approach is usually a bit more nuanced. We've already referenced the hypothetical fabrications that are made up to gloss over the scandal of Jesus' family tree. But when it comes to story details, rather than simply changing a number to fall in line with a hypothetical original, a more complex approach is taken. When a story is repeated twice and contradictions are evident, the two accounts are usually weaved together to construct a synthesis.

That most famous of Jesus' sermons is a great example. Even though Christian tradition has assigned different titles to Matthew's version and Luke's version, calling the former the "Sermon on the Mount" and the latter the "Sermon on the Plain," their similarities usually lead scholars to conclude that they originate from the same source and that they are in essence the same sermon. The similarities in message content are just too striking to presume otherwise. Especially since the gospels of Matthew and Luke share so many stories between them. Yet the differences are striking as well. In addition to the conflicts in location and posture mentioned earlier, the sermons are recorded in markedly distinct fashion. *How shall we reconcile these accounts in order to defend them as flawless? How can the same sermon be recorded word for word and result in two entirely different manuscripts?*

Evangelical teaching gets right to work with almost effortless ease. Here we watch the masters of harmonization on the top of their game: if Luke says Jesus "came down with them and stood on a level place" and Matthew writes that Jesus "went up on a mountain, and when he sat down, his disciples came to him," these events actually can be synthesized. Rather easily, in fact. Just use a touch of creativity and think of the big picture event, while approaching each detail in minimalist terms. Take into account what the narrative *does* say as well as what it *doesn't*.

That's a key tool for the toolbox, right there. Approach each of the story's details in minimalist terms and feel free to expand upon what's not explicitly limited. That way you create larger gaps in the story, allowing you to more easily fit the two accounts together and also hypothesize additional details to help smooth them out.

For instance, returning to these two sermons. Luke never says Jesus stood the *whole* time. And it doesn't say *where* the level place was located. All we have to say is that within the rather hilly somewhat mountainous region of Israel, Jesus "went up on a mountain" and then eventually "came down" a little ways further, finding a "level place" or a plateau of sorts *within* the mountainous area. So now he's both "up on the mountain" and "down on a level place" at the same time. Then you just have to say that some of the sermon, maybe the first part, was delivered while he was seated as the disciples that had already followed him up on the hill then more closely gather around him. But at another part of the sermon, maybe the second part, Jesus "stood" during his teaching.

Boom! Bang! Voilà!

Biblical harmony!

Or an even simpler way to approach these sermons is to do as I did in my teaching. As a pastor-teacher, I speculated two things. First, that like many traveling teachers, Jesus spoke on many common themes throughout his itinerant ministry and that he was known for using several illustrations and parables repeatedly among his varying crowds. Therefore, it would make sense for him to have two completely different events with very similar yet verbally distinct sermons.

Second, I would often suggest that Matthew's and Luke's intentions were that these accounts (along with others that fill the gospels' pages) not necessarily be understood as time-and-place events but rather as synopses of the whole of Jesus' teaching ministry. Since evangelical theology typically anchors inerrancy with *authorial intent*, this approach works well among evangelicals. Events are only to be understood literally to the extent of the authors' intentions.

But either way, whether one attempts to synthesize accounts or to argue against an unwelcome modernist literalism, biblical credibility would be defended. Scenarios like this often find skeptics so confident in their critique of inerrancy and then shocked at how easily evangelical belief continues. Meanwhile believers laugh at how effortlessly they are able to defend the legitimacy of God's Word against unwarranted attack.

Never underestimate the determined creativity of the evangelical mind.

Consider the contradiction of Jesus' robe color, which evangelicals try to resolve using an unusual method.

Critics of the Bible lay their argument down: the account is of an event that clearly only happened once, the crucifixion, so you can't say it was two different robes worn at two different times. Matthew 27 says the Roman soldiers "stripped him and put a scarlet robe on him," while John 19 says they "arrayed him in a purple robe." *So which is it?* Clearly these are different colors. "Purple" and "violet" may overlap. Or "scarlet" and "red." But either it's scarlet or it's purple here. Not both.

Or at least that's what someone reading without bias would conclude. But here the typical seminary-fed answer I received and then passed along to my congregation was that the color described likely does not speak of an inherent quality of the robe itself but of how it *appeared* to witnesses. Since the context shows readers the purpose of the robe was to mock Jesus as a self-proclaimed king, complete with thorn crown and reed scepter, it is likely that the robe was actually a royal purple. But given the vantage point of some observers and maybe just the way the sun was streaming through any cloud cover—giving a particular mix of visual contrast, brightness, and reflection—it would seem plausible that observers could see his robe as a scarlet one. And maybe God would superintend Jesus' robe to appear scarlet to some, even as a confirmation that his scarlet blood was about to be shed for all humanity. *And now there you have it!* From the perspective of some onlookers, the robe was purple, and from the perspective of others, it appeared scarlet! Both are correct in their own way!

But there's a problem with this line of defense, you see.

If the Bible is believed to present inerrant truth, then we have to admit that Jesus' robe had a true color. It was either purple or scarlet or it was green or blue. But it was not both. Not inherently. Not *truly*. The biblical text does not say that they put on a robe that *appeared* scarlet. No, it says they put a robe on him that was actually scarlet. Plain and simple. Regardless of how the robe is *perceived*, it has a true inherent color, and that color is said to be two different qualities that simply do not overlap.

Even better, if we nonetheless content ourselves in saying that the Bible is merely saying it is "true" to the mere extent of *perception* rather than *reality*, if we soften the Bible's sense of inerrancy in such a way, the effects here are catastrophic for the biblical literalist. This then forces the evangelical to acknowledge the same soft inerrancy to all of the Bible's teaching. It then becomes true that John *perceives* Jesus to be the Son of God and that Paul *perceives* Jesus' sacrifice to have paid for the sins of the world, but this no longer says anything about *actual reality*, only religious perception or symbolism. Either that or Jesus wore two different robes. But you can't have it both ways.

On to solving our fourth New Testament inconsistency. We saw earlier that Matthew, Luke, and John each record a completely different set of words by Jesus that is followed by a statement of his subsequent death. In each account, Jesus makes his statement, and then as Luke puts it, "having said this he breathed his last." But again, evangelicals can harmonize this by reading creatively and minimally. Between Jesus' action of speaking and his action of dying, no one would deny the presence of at least a fraction of a second. Maybe even several seconds. If several seconds elapsed between Jesus speaking and his final breath, would it render Luke's words any less true? What if several minutes elapsed? Would this be impossibly outside the function of Luke's words? And honestly, within the big picture of this story that unfolds over tens of hours, couldn't Jesus have spoken those words and then taken another hour to really breathe his last breath? Yet, one could still truthfully observe, "After several hours of torment, Jesus called out in a loud voice and said, 'Father, into your hands I commit my spirit!' And having said this [an hour later] he breathed his last." The argument can be made that Jesus' last breath could have taken place within a window of time that is larger than just a few seconds while still maintaining the literal inerrancy of Luke's words.

Now take that one step further. If there may have been more than a mere couple seconds between the recorded words and his final breath, certainly there may have been other events and actions that took place within that same space of time. Maybe Jesus even said *a little bit more* after the phrase that Luke latched onto. Maybe he simply groaned. Or maybe he said, "Goodbye Mom," in a barely audible voice. Or maybe he said the other two statements that the gospels of Matthew and John record. Maybe, in effect, all three of these were his "last words." And maybe it didn't even require an hour of time to do so. Maybe it took only about ninety seconds. Jesus cries out in a loud voice, "My God, my God, why have you forsaken me?" followed by another loud cry, say twenty seconds later, "Father, into your hands I commit my spirit!" and then a minute after that, just as those last syllables struggle from his lips, "It is finished." Couldn't all of these honestly be claimed by Jesus' followers as among his last words? *And so they are.*

And the evangelicals scoff once more at the attacks of their detractors.

This kind of harmonization is foundational to systematic theology, taking phrases and concepts from all over the Bible and piecing them together into a whole. Once you get the hang of this kind of approach, almost any disparate details can be smoothed over. Synthesis. Taking all elements from both versions of the story and weaving them together to create a third.

But while this approach "verifies" the literal details of both versions, doesn't it actually end up creating an entirely other account? It fashions a third story, a version of the event that one would never envision by simply reading the Bible's own words. You have to ask yourself, *If God wanted you to see the third synthesized version as the true one, wouldn't he have just written that one down instead?* What kind of divine communicator tells half-stories that lead you to naturally envision at face value something other than what it actually was? What kind of divine communicator communicates so vaguely that factions of his followers are forced to spend centuries warring over conflicting interpretations?

Now, I promised you at the start of this chapter that we'd end with a big contradiction that I didn't really face off against until my faith was already near the point of unravel. We'll call this one The Big Daddy.

The Big Daddy: Judas Iscariot's Death Tale

And now we move to what may require the greatest feat of harmonization ever imagined. The longest stretch of all. Taking the two accounts of Judas Iscariot's death and blending them into one seamless narrative. And as I mentioned earlier, this is the one that eventually helped push me over the edge to admit to myself how completely ridiculous our efforts had become. I taught this stuff for years, but a single skeptical response from one church member stunned me to silence.

First, the evangelical act of harmonization.

As mentioned, we have the contradicting accounts from the Gospel of Matthew and the book of Acts. See what we have in the text:

Account One: Matthew 27:3–10

Then when Judas, his betrayer, saw that Jesus was condemned, he changed his mind and brought back the thirty pieces of silver to the chief priests and the elders, saying, "I have sinned by betraying innocent blood." They said, "What is that to us? See to it yourself." And throwing down the pieces of silver into the temple, he departed, and he went and hanged himself. But the chief priests, taking the pieces of silver, said, "It is not lawful to put them into the treasury, since it is blood money." So they took counsel and bought with them the potter's field as a burial place for strangers. Therefore that field has been called the Field of Blood to this day. Then was fulfilled what had been spoken by the prophet Jeremiah, saying, "And they took the thirty pieces of silver, the price of him on whom a price had been set by some of the sons of Israel, and they gave them for the potter's field, as the Lord directed me."

Account Two: Acts 1:18–19

Now this man bought a field with the reward of his wickedness, and falling headlong he burst open in the middle and all his bowels gushed out. And it became known to all the inhabitants of Jerusalem, so that the field was called in their own language Akeldama, that is, Field of Blood.

Though the evangelical has his work cut out for him in approaching these two passages, he tackles it with vigor. The question is raised. *How can these passages possibly be harmonized?* They clearly look like two completely different accounts, campfire stories handed down in almost legendary fashion. Though someone could make the case that one of these accounts reflects reality, surely it could only be one—not both. *Aren't the differences between these two simply too big to reconcile?*

But once again, we cannot be so naïve. The evangelical is committed to inerrancy, and he will find a way to harmonize the accounts. We take the apparently opposing data and set them side by side. In Matthew, Judas returns the silver and the elders use it to purchase the potter's field. In Acts, Judas uses the silver to buy the potter's field himself. In Matthew, Judas leaves the temple and hangs himself, but in Acts, he falls to the ground in his new field and hits his head while his midsection bursts open and his bowels gush out. In Matthew, the field is nicknamed "Field of Blood" because the elders had repurposed it as a burial ground for foreigners. In Acts, the reason for the nickname is because it's the place where Judas is known to have fallen and died. So many contradictions, made so sincerely. What are biblicists to do?

Here's how I as a pastor handled the discrepancies: Judas must have returned to the temple guilt-ridden, having betrayed an innocent man, and thrown the silver to the floor, wanting nothing to do with his blood money. Then, despairing of life and not knowing what to do, he stumbled out to a local potter's field (possibly a little drunk), where he attempted to hang himself from a tree in that very field. But, as he was hanging himself from that tree, the rope must have broken (or maybe the branch), casting him with such great force to the ground that he flipped head over heels, hitting his head on the ground while also violently pushing his midsection into a rock. This collision in turn split his belly open and his intestines literally spilled all over the earth. At this point Judas was dead (both by hanging *and* by falling headlong), but the field still technically belonged to the potter. Having discovered what happened with Judas, the elders must have suddenly realized what they needed to do with the silver. They rushed out to purchase the field from the potter using the blood money. Acquiring the field with Judas' money and in Judas' name, they backdated the purchase to ensure that the records showed he had already owned the land prior to death. Thus, we can both say that the elders purchased the field and claim that in a sense Judas did as well. The elders then saw to it that the field would be repurposed as an immigrant burial ground. Over time, the field was given the name "Field of Blood." Some people called it this because they knew of Judas' death, but others called it by the same name simply because it was a burial ground. Now we've created a plausible scenario for how there are two different reasons behind the field's name.

And *voilà!*

We now have a single story that includes every detail from both accounts, with each of the biblical stories only including the specific details that best serve their divinely inspired purposes. I suggested that it actually made sense that each author edited out some details. After all, no written account includes every detail of all that goes on in real life. And I was never insistent that my proposed synthesis had to be the correct one. I simply showed that such a synthesis was possible. These discrepancies need not shake our faith, I would say.

And yet, I think for most evangelical readers, there's this "matter of the gut"—a sense of discomfort throughout this whole process. The details of these two stories are *very* different. Too different. Significantly beyond a few stray details or shades of color. They are two completely different stories written in a way that creates vastly different scenarios in the minds of their readers. And so as evangelicals, there comes this point where we must ask ourselves, *Are we really being honest with the text? And with ourselves?*

That is precisely the level of discomfort we experienced one night as we walked through these two texts at a Bible study. I had taught my synthesis as explained above for years, and it was always received with affirmative nods as Bible students scribbled the details down and into the margins of their Bibles.

But this night was different. Toward the end of my tenure as pastor at West Hills Church and as my faith was increasingly suffering cracks in its walls, a group of about twelve had gathered at someone's home. We were studying the events surrounding the crucifixion when conversation settled upon the conditions of Judas Iscariot's death. When we read the two accounts side by side, the women and men present were clearly troubled by the differences between them. They were caught off guard and more than a little shocked, never having quite compared the two stories side by side and never having realized how glaringly contradictory they were. But as the leader of the Bible study, I guided the group as we began to process what we saw in the text. I reminded everyone of the inerrancy of God's Word and suggested that these were simply two sides of the same story. I then suggested the very same synthesis I just offered above.

But the response was not as I had expected. So taken aback by the plainly ridiculous nature of my synthesis, the entire group fell silent. Visibly wearied by the obstacle course I had pushed them through, their wide eyes drifted between one another around the circle of the group. I also remained silent, allowing everyone time to process and waiting for their thoughts. Finally one member suggested an alternative. "Or . . . maybe this is simply two different authors just trying to say that Judas died? And maybe the specific stories don't have to be reconciled?" He elaborated, "Maybe we can just call it a literary technique or poetic license, simply portraying the basic fact that 'Judas died.' To that end, they are both correct. Do the details really matter?" Everyone immediately began nodding their heads in agreement that his suggestion was much more plausible than the preposterous gallimaufry I had just offered.

I wanted to raise the concerns that his theory brings: these passages aren't poetic and give no signs of anything but a literal account of Judas' life. No indications are present that would tip the gauge of authorial intent in any other direction. I wanted to raise issues of biblical inerrancy and of every word of each account necessarily having to be correct. I wanted to raise these issues. I genuinely and instinctively *wanted* to. I felt the pastoral obligation to not let potential heresy continue unidentified. But I didn't. I *couldn't*. I didn't and couldn't because I too knew that the synthesis sounded lunatic. It sounded truly ridiculous. It didn't make sense. And as much as I felt compelled to defend the purity of God's Word, inwardly I fell crippled. I feared my own sense of logic was being betrayed by a lacking theology, and I suddenly felt I no longer knew how to respond. *How could I defend a defenseless idea?*

This was the first and only time in all my years of ministry that I absolutely didn't know how to respond. In the hundreds of Bible studies I had led that all featured group discussion and in the countless hours of open question-and-answer sessions, this was the first time I had fallen completely silent. Vocally immobilized. I had had an answer in my arsenal, but I then realized it to be pathetically inadequate. So after a brief moment of pause, I transitioned and moved on with the study, my soul defeated. I felt defeated not by the alternative our friend had suggested, but rather defeated by the Bible's own lack of cohesion.

It would be a mistake to now assume that Judas Iscariot's death tale is what sent me over the edge and killed my faith in Jesus. It would also be a mistake to assume that it served as a final last straw of sorts that jammed my desk drawer open. But it and all of these examples did sit in the back of my mind marinating over the course of nearly twenty years. It was only later in ministry and in collaboration with other bigger challenges to my faith that the Judas inconsistency was suddenly raised and then less easily filed away. But we'll get to more of all that a little later.

The bigger point here is to bring us all into greater conversation with one another. *Are the evangelicals in the room able to take a step back and see why some of this stuff looks so ridiculous to those who do not already have a bias toward things of conservative Christian faith? And are the atheists and other skeptics in the room able to more fully understand and even appreciate what enables evangelicals to explain away criticisms with what feels like a rational and sane approach?*

Think about it this way. If all we knew of my story was what's been shared so far, wouldn't it kind of make sense that I continued to file my questions away? In the sixth grade, I pray for God to relieve me of the desire to end my life and *poof!*—all such desires disappear in a literal instant. I pray other big prayers that seem to be answered with only one possible explanation. All the while I am surrounded by a community and church context, have a career and Bible-college education, in which good things are repeatedly associated with faith in Jesus. And so, yes, maybe there're a few glaring discrepancies within our Bible, I'd reason. Maybe it doesn't all make perfect sense to us mere humans. But I trusted in the God who had transformed my life, and a few scholarly conundrums couldn't deny the real-life change I'd personally experienced.

And so, in this context, *of course* the Judas conundrum isn't going to shipwreck one's faith overnight.

But this isn't the entire context.
And our story is far from over.

Questions for the Dialogue

This chapter's final section already posed a couple direct questions to help kick-start the dialogue. We'll reiterate them below and add several more to the mix.

For Believing Christians

- Of the five sets of Old Testament contradictions, which if any were you already aware of?

    1. Second Samuel 24 v. First Chronicles 21 (Punishment Timeline)
    2. First Kings 4 v. Second Chronicles 9 (Number of Horse Stalls)
    3. Second Kings 8 v. Second Chronicles 22 (Age Ahaziah Became King)
    4. First Kings 16 v. Second Chronicles 16 (Year of Baasha's Death)
    5. Second Kings 24 v. Second Chronicles 36 (Age Jehoiachin Became King)

- Of the five sets of New Testament contradictions, which if any were you already aware of?

    1. Matthew 1 v. Luke 3 (Genealogies)
    2. Matthew 5–7 v. Luke 6 (Sermon Particulars)
    3. Matthew 27 v. John 19 (Robe Color)
    4. Matthew 27 v. Luke 23 v. John 19 (Jesus' Last Words)
    5. Matthew 27 v. Acts 1 (Judas Iscariot's Death)

- What's your reaction when reading about these inconsistencies? Are any surprising to you? How so?

- Within your Christian social circle, do you currently feel free to share fully your reactions publicly? If anyone were to express doubt in the Bible's credibility, how would people respond? Why do you think this is?

- Do you personally believe that the Christian Bible is inerrant? If so, how do you justify this belief in light of these and other contradictions? Is there any hypothetical discovery someone could make tomorrow that would convince you that your Bible wasn't actually from God? If not, does this reveal an element of bias on your part and is that acceptable to you?

- Imagine yourself as someone who comes from another religion. How easily do you think they would be convinced that the Christian Bible is the perfect Word of God?

- Are you able to take a step back and understand why inconsistencies like these might make it harder for some people to believe that the Bible is inerrant?

For Atheists and Skeptics

- What's your big takeaway from this chapter? Were any of the contradictions in the Christian Bible surprising to you? Were they more or less blatant than you were expecting?

- Were you surprised by the process evangelicals take to explain away their Bible's inconsistencies? How might this differ from previous assumptions?

- How might you find yourself systematizing the world around you in a way that is similar to the evangelical's practice of systematic theology? To what extent might it appear from their perspective like this is a reasonable process?

- Imagine yourself as a devout lifelong believer. How difficult do you think it would be to accept criticism of the Bible?

- Prior to reading this, had you been frustrated by how easily evangelicals seem to trust in their Bible even though it's full of contradictions? And after reading this, does their devotion make more or less sense to you?

- Are you able to take a step back and understand or even appreciate how evangelical Christians are able to dismiss the Bible's contradictions and remain convinced of its inerrancy?

PART THREE:
THE FALL OF EVERYTHING
I HAD EVER KNOWN

Chapter Seven

Snowball:
A Cartoon Character Rolling Down a Hill of Doom

Let's begin with a warm Sunday morning in the September of 2010. I was all set to preach on one of my favorite topics: the grand and epic forward thrust of God's redemptive plan for humanity. Pastors often like to talk about how they interpret the Bible's many prophetic verses on future events, and my sermons were commonly peppered with themes of those coming days as well.

But contrary to what might make for traditional interpretations, I saw in the Bible's imagery and terminology a future "heaven" that would be a bright and vibrant urban community—*seriously, an actual city that would feel even more real life than Chicago does today*—hustling and bustling with activity where every one of its citizens were both servants and royalty all at the same time, simultaneously lowering themselves before others as selfless servants in the likeness of Jesus while also being exalted in return by those same others as children of the Great King. Patterned after Jesus himself, who was both King of Kings and the Sacrificial Lamb who put the needs of the world before his own, we too would form the kind of community where every single resident reflected both his royalty and his self-sacrificing servanthood all at the same time and bound together as one. A great big city that was completely composed of princes and princesses all taking turns serving one another in humility and joy.

It was to be highly active and relational and interactive and other-focused. And our service toward one another would be done in devotion to Yahweh our

Great King. Heaven would not be composed of a silent inner worship of God while kneeling on clouds or playing harps with angels. We had never been created to live this life alone, so why would our eternity be any different? Thus, our eternal worship was to be an inherently social experience. It was the culmination of The Story of God and Humanity, and it was to be an eternal overflow of laughter and joy and peace and of the most vibrant of community.

But it would all begin with what was referred to as The Restoration. This would be that future point where Jesus would return to bridge this earthen life with that one. It was the point where this coming Prince of Peace and King of Kings was to finally recreate and glorify everything in his image, returning it to be "exactly as it was always intended to be."

I really truly believed these things and was so enthralled by the perfected bliss that would await us on that glorious day that it would even drive me to tears. I found society's brokenness heart-wrenching and longed for the arrival of God's transformational healing upon all humanity. I was beyond confident that it was "only a matter of time," as they say, and fully trusted that even now God was working behind the scenes to orchestrate events and connect dots in anticipation of the healing restoration that would one day burst forth.

And so it was on this warm Sunday morning in the September of 2010 that I delivered a pretty fantastic sermon along these very lines. Got rave and emotional reviews.

I had worked toward the sermon's conclusion by recapping various fairytales. The ones involving princesses locked in towers and entranced with sleep. The ones with dragons and witches. The ones where the prince has to fight all odds of challenge and obstacle. But the ones where finally in the end, the prince defeats the dragon and saves the princess. The ones in which that day really does finally and actually come. And where the prince and his bride then live happily ever after.

And of course we reminded ourselves that morning of the Bible's descriptions, that it speaks of the devil as a dragon and of the church as a bride, of how Jesus is the prince of heaven, and of how one day that prince would return to rescue his bride the church and take her home forever, back to his Father's house in the city of radiance.

And as we were working our way through the talk and as the level of emotional intensity was building higher and ever higher, and as the imagery of dragons and dark magic gave way to that of returning princes and rescued maidens, we ended with this: the wondrous reality that though the Grand and Epic Story of God and Humanity was like the best of fairytales, it yet remained profoundly more than *just* a fairytale. That in reality, our story would not close as we looked once again out our windows to a war-torn world of greed, isolation, and injustice. That in Jesus, the prince really will return for his bride. That in Jesus, we really will live happily ever after. That in Jesus, none of this is too good to be true. And that the reason it isn't too good to be true is because *in Jesus, fairytales really do become reality*.

The end.

And the crowd went wild.

However, there was one problem.

The problem is that while I was preaching this magnificent sermon's fantastic conclusion, my brain glitched. Oh, all the words came out okay. No perceived irregularities. But somehow in my brain there was a glitch that managed to twist an ankle.

See, when I got to the part where I proclaimed that *in Jesus fairytales really do become reality*, this terrifying thought entered my mind. Just this little train wreck of a split-second flash of insight occurred.

It said: *What if the fact that it sounds too good to be true is reason enough to think that it might be? And what if the reason it sounds like a fairytale is because it too is nothing more than a product of human invention and idealism? And what if the only reason I'm preaching this is because Jesus himself actually is a fairytale but I'm just too blind to recognize it?*

Damn.

Right there in the middle of the room standing before all these people, I actually had those thoughts. Time almost seemed to freeze for the moment. I swear, the clock itself almost stopped right then and there.

But even as quickly as these momentary questions flashed through my mind, I abruptly dismissed them as the lies of the devil that I knew them to be. And so, out of sight they were pushed, and to the desk drawer they were just as quickly cast.

I did after all have a worship event to wrap up—and a whole room full of hands waiting to be shaken.

When God Neglects His Promises

The fairytale of returning future kings wasn't the only belief beginning to unravel. In the months surrounding that month of September, I started seeing little holes beginning to break open across my faith like Swiss cheese on rye. Yes, there was an increased and frustrating awareness of the kinds of biblical flaws that we've already discussed at length. But in those months my concerns and frustrations began growing far beyond those regarding biblical credibility. And those concerns became channels that opened up increasing layers of doubt-laced question marks.

Rising as chief among them all was a problem related to how the Christian church behaved around the world and throughout history. You know, all the murders and rapes and tortures and wars and crusades done in the name of the Christian god, terrible horrible things that started way back at basically the beginning of Christianity and have continued ever since. But my problem went far beyond simple disillusionment with the church itself. My problem was with the idea that God was said to indwell his people for the explicit purpose of ensuring that they acted the way he wanted them to—and yet he had seemed to let them do pretty much whatever the hell they wanted, apparently without correction and absent of concern.

Now the standard line of response from evangelicals is this. Since Christians are in the process of redemption, *it only makes sense* that some of those who are earlier in that redemptive process still do some pretty nasty things. On top of this you also have the evangelical argument that the only true segment of Christianity is the one holding evangelical beliefs. So they would suggest that *it only makes sense* for other parts of Christianity to do horrible crimes, since they weren't or aren't truly Christian anyway.

And in declaring truth as such, they take God off the hook from all the bad things of the world, even those done by the very individuals who thought they were doing it out of allegiance to him in the first place.

But this is where it was becoming quite problematic for me. In other words, I began having a hard time buying the clichéd evangelical line of response. You see, in the summer of 2010, I had worked my way through an up-close look at the New Testament book of Ephesians. And after studying it relentlessly and thinking through its implications ceaselessly for months on end, I began to find some of its promises a bit unsettling.

In Ephesians we find God making all these huge promises concerning his plans for the Christian church. Beyond all the imagery of the second chapter where it says that God has united all the church's various segments into one indivisible community, it then outlines in the fourth a long list of promises that God is said to have committed himself to achieving within that indivisible church. And there it is said that by his indwelling Holy Spirit, God Himself would embody both the universal church as a whole and each individual within it for the explicit purpose of preserving and transforming each of Jesus' followers into everything they were ever intended to be, without exception.

And it's there in Ephesians 4 where God promises that he would provide a steady stream of human church leaders who would be empowered by this indwelling Holy Spirit to build the entire global Christian church into a flawlessly united faith that is built on their perfected knowledge of Jesus as God's Son. Ephesians goes on to promise that this would ensure that all Christians would grow up into a mature faith, never to ever again be confused or tricked by false teaching. And it says that God had taken steps to ensure that if at any point in its future history, erroneous or heretical teachings should arise within the church, that those teachings would be squelched away by a guaranteed-to-be-faithful leadership. Erroneous teachings may arise from time to time, it says, but God had promised that his unified church would be a place of stability where waves and winds of misunderstanding, error, and deceit would be calmed and removed. God had promised to make Christianity the shining beacon of unity and truth and love for all the earth to see.

In other words, in Ephesians 4 God had clearly promised to feed perfected truth to his followers and had personally guaranteed that he would use his supernatural indwelling to make sure everyone in the historic, global church believed correctly.

Full and complete organizational unity.

In God-perfected, safeguarded, and complete truth.

Without exception.

And yet. And yet as I looked around at the world today and throughout history, one thing was clear. At no point in any of the church's lineage has any of these promises ever come even close to fruition. In fact, the church just seems to get more and more fragmented as the timeline progresses. Our plethora of Christian denominations certainly seem to find very little to agree upon. I mean, they can't even agree on who exactly Jesus was, which you'd think would be the most important detail of all for God to supernaturally and universally nail down. It's bad enough when you look at how splintered Christianity's segments and local churches are, but when you then consider the diverse perspectives of the individuals within each local church, it becomes an endless web of shattered and speculative theology.

And so as I returned to those very words of Ephesians in the fall of 2010, I simply found it impossible to rationalize away the weight of God's promises. God had promised to unite every individual in truth and yet they were all divided. The great global and historic church of God had spent centuries pillaging and infighting and crusading and raping even as they couldn't even agree on something so foundational as the identity of Jesus Christ. And it all took place on God's watch and under his oversight. Something wasn't right. Something was *terribly wrong.*

Comparisons to Other Religions Can Only Make Things Worse

Before long, question marks started popping up everywhere I looked. And at times I would wonder: *What if I had been a Muslim?* I would actually, literally ask this of myself.

And you'll see why I asked this of myself in a moment.

Beginning with the early days of my evangelism training as a teenager, I had been taught principles in how to help adherents of other religions think through the evidence of Christianity so that they might come to see its "truth." This featured identifying the cognitive weak points of whatever their own religion may have been. But it also intended to bring them to a point of emotional and social strength where they would be able to let go of the flawed religious thinking they had grown up with and to embrace the truth of Christianity without bias.

I grew up practicing and rehearsing my interactions with those of various perspectives and would role-play the conversations we might share, getting my points down, my arguments, and my apologetic. And it was all in an effort to help my would-be conversationalists see the weakness and bias in their own perspectives, to free them up so they would then accept and embrace my own.

I would try to, *as they say*, put myself in their shoes. I'd work to feel what they might feel and to envision life as they might see it. I would often wonder what it would take to convince a lifelong Hindu that their Hindu beliefs and perspective were flawed and that they should embrace the Christian beliefs and perspective instead. And what would it take to convince the same of a Buddhist? What about for a Jew or a Muslim or an atheist? What would it take to liberate an encaged mind that had grown up just assuming that the religion of one's heritage and culture was the correct one—*when it wasn't?*

I had been thinking those thoughts for nearly twenty years.

And then one day I looked in the proverbial mirror.

And I wondered if it could possibly be true that the only reason I had believed the truth of Christianity for as long as I had was because it was simply the religion of *my own* heritage and culture. For no other reason than that *I* was born into it.

Just as a Hindu in a Hindu community.

Or a Buddhist in a Buddhist community.

Or a Jewish person in a Jewish community.

Or just as a Muslim in a Muslim community.

And I then began to wonder what *I* would need to hear in order to convince me that I had until now been wrong. *Even hypothetically.* What kind of argument would it take to convince *me*? And what would *I* be willing to hear? Or was I so biased in *my* assumptions that I wouldn't even be willing to consider any alternatives, regardless of how sound their arguments against me might be?

How could I ever expect a Muslim or Buddhist to be willing to pursue truth beyond their religion if I wasn't willing to pursue truth beyond mine? There had to be an objective standard against which all religions, including my own, could be measured against. And only those matching that standard could be considered valid.

But it simply wasn't logical to base beliefs on feelings or comforts. That's what I had always told the adherents of other religions. *And it's what I now knew I had to tell myself.*

It's true that my faith "just felt right" to me. But couldn't Muslims say the same about theirs?

It's true that my faith brought me a level of inner comfort. But again couldn't Muslims claim the same as well?

It's true that I had always attributed good things in my life with blessings for following my faith while also attributing the bad as the consequences of rebellion. But here too, wouldn't Muslims believe the same?

Don't we both credit our prayers for the healing we discover? And when those prayers result in more sickness and even death, don't we both explain it away as God's will being more important than our own?

To move beyond some of this, evangelicals love to hold up religious uniqueness as a test of truth. Christianity must be true, it's said, because no other religion is as unique in the world as Christianity. It's the only one with a god who incarnates himself or the only one with a god who sacrifices his son (or himself) for his people or the only one with a god that rises from the dead or the only one that promises a salvation which comes by simple faith alone or—*on and on and on the list goes.*

But then I came to see that there were segments of Buddhism and Hinduism and the countless religious myths of myriad ancient traditions that portrayed the exact same concepts as Christianity but from a much earlier time. And I came to see that Christianity really wasn't at all unique compared to other world religions, at least not any more unique than *each of them were* in regard to the others. Yes, each one was *different.* But they were all *equally* different. Christianity really had no award-winning lead on differences.

So why did I believe?

Why did I believe in the Christian Bible?
And why did I believe in its god?

And so in the fall of 2010 the long list of questions began lining up and packing in around me. Everywhere I turned, I started seeing frustrations, problems, and inconsistencies that plagued my sense of reason. As the theological and biblical conundrums I faced continued to amass, so too did my questions about the simple and basic functioning of Christianity and its leaders.

We're talking about pastors exploiting emotions to gain religious conversions while then turning around to rail against those very same emotions as evil and in need of suppression. We're talking about pastors making promises that new converts will be filled with an unending flood of wonder and joy while then turning around to tell them afterward that this joy will be denied them until they're in heaven. We're talking about pastors proclaiming that Jesus' followers only need enough faith to match the smallest of seeds while then turning around to blame the depression and addiction and poverty of the depressed, addicted, and impoverished on the smallness of their faith.

And on top of it all, the thing that continued to drive me the most crazy was that in response to how completely messed up this long line of common pastoral manipulations was, *God did absolutely nothing about it to set the record straight.*

Some may promise that God will indeed set the record straight, but that he is simply waiting do so until the end of days when all is transitioned unto eternity. That he is holding off right now in order to test the faith of his followers, in order to see whose faith is true and whose isn't. And that if he were to set the record straight right now, it would make our faith too easy, too simple, too material. That if God came down to set the record straight, it would actually *undermine* the development of a robust faith.

I'd think about that line of reasoning.

And then I'd be reminded of how God actually does things in the Bible.

That in the Bible God comes down to set the record straight over and over and over again. That God comes down to set the record straight if his humans do so much as hold a wooden pole the wrong way. And that he does so visually, physically, audibly, and usually with a great gust of arson. Not naturally but *supernaturally.*

And then I'd wonder if the Muslim makes similar excuses for why their version of God hasn't come down physically to set the record straight against Christianity.

I'd wonder again what it would take to convince the Muslim of the truth of Christianity.

I'd wonder what it would take to convince me of the truth of Islam. *What would it take to convince me of anything?*

Truth at All Costs

I'd often hear my grandfather's words replaying in the back of my mind. You remember him, the homespun fundamentalist who had so deeply shaped my faith. He had always taught me to seek truth above and before the opinions of others. He had taught me to disregard tradition for tradition's sake and to always be skeptical of any religious leader no matter how many theological degrees they may have attained.

Truth first, he would say.

Be ruthless in its pursuit, he would say.

Truth before tradition. Truth before any particular church or its leaders. Truth even before family, he would say.

I love that man dearly. He has arguably been the fiercest advocate for Christian faith in my life, and yet his words were ones that ultimately drove me beyond it. One day in the near future I would be sitting in my living room contemplating whether my pursuit of truth could be worth leaving Christianity. His words would come to mind. And his words in particular would give me the final push. *To pursue truth at all costs, no matter the wreckage that may be left in its wake.*

And so as you might expect, this all began to snowball quite quickly. Like one of those rapidly growing monster snowballs chasing you down a classic *Looney Toons* mountain, the whole thing was growing rapidly out of control.

I had just seen way too much. And the more I noticed, the less I could ignore. I had often felt like Dorothy in *The Wizard of Oz*. Like after spending time in the presence of the Great and Powerful One, I had caught an unexpected glimpse behind the curtain to discover the whole thing was just a sham, the product of a desperate humanity bumbling around and pulling at levers.

And now that I had seen it, I couldn't unsee it. But the truth is that I had really liked my faith. The worldview it had created for me was comfortable. It was a world where I was right in the center of a divine plan that seemed to have my best interest in mind. It was a world that had guaranteed me an amazing future filled with joy and purpose and peace and community. It was an exciting adventure. And it was safe. And now this world was fading away. And I was being left alone to fend for myself.

I desperately wanted to close my eyes to this growing realization. I wanted to close my eyes and wish everything back to the way it was. I wanted to crawl back into the comforts of my faith.

Basically I just wanted God to be real again.

But my eyes had been opened. And they now refused to close. That bottom right-hand desk drawer had been opened, and *it* now refused to close. It was as if I came to a point where the back corners of my mind refused to let me believe in God any further, as if the reality of a godless world had so completely saturated my awareness that my mind now said, *"Nope, not gonna let you believe it anymore! Open your eyes and look around. I won't let you escape this!"*

After years of accumulation, I had reached a point of mental inability to further suppress what was growing more obvious by the week. I had lost all ability to power down the feed of skepticism now churning diligently in the forefront of my mind. And what's more, now that all those puzzling questions were pulled up and laid out across the desktop in front of me, my mind automatically began experimenting with how the pieces might best fit together once we take God out of the equation.

The reassembly was effortless.

And I found its ease terrifying.

A clear and easy set of answers began to emerge: that all we see and encounter in nature seems explainable by quite natural means; that there's no compelling reason to assume another realm of existence beyond this one; that there's no need to fill gaps of knowledge with magical thinking or mythical assumptions; that there no longer seemed any good reason to believe in the existence of any god whatsoever.

In other words, that if I had grown up without any religious orientation, there was absolutely nothing that would naturally lead me to conclude on my own that my god or any other god would likely exist. I had realized that if it were not for my own personal bias, it would seem objectively clear that all the gods of human history were fiction. Including my own. It had become clear that I was becoming an atheist.

And yet somehow I knew I wasn't ready to give up on God just yet. Despite all that my head was telling me, I couldn't let it go. I just couldn't.

So even as my mind was realizing the impossibility of my faith, my heart continued clinging to it, demanding its resurgence, and refusing to give up. And so the more the cognitive evidence mounted against the reality of God's existence, the more my heart ran frantically in search of the love of its youth.

What resulted was a civil war of the psyche.

Forcing Crazy Will Drive You Insane

There's this moment in the 2016 Netflix documentary *Tony Robbins: I Am Not Your Guru* where Robbins is coaching an unspeakably broken woman in the audience of one of his conferences. She had been through a thoroughly horrific experience growing up within a sadistic Christian cult, suffering virtually every form of abuse known to humanity. If you can imagine it, she's been subjected to it. Repeatedly. And now she's spent her entire adult life freed of the cult but still trapped in its psychological aftermath. She wants full freedom but just can't shake these events of the past and how they were allowed to happen. And then there's this point where Tony breaks in and tells her something powerful. He says, "You've been trying to make sense of all this. But there is no sense. And that's what's made you the most crazy."

Thankfully, few of us have endured the level of abuse that this woman has. Yet, Robbins' words can ring true for many of us on several levels as we try to force reason into an unreasonable belief system.

Trying to make sense of what doesn't make sense will make you crazy.

And I was at a point in the fall of 2010 where I was spending all day every day trying to make sense of why God wasn't restoring my faith even though I so desperately wanted him to. The Bible promised that God would always grant us faith if we asked, yet I was asking and he wasn't granting. This tension had become the constant white noise in the back of my mind from sunrise to sunset and each moment thereafter.

For several years I had long enjoyed a Christian practice known as *ceaseless prayer*. It's where you establish a constant inner dialogue, forming all your thoughts, musings, desires, and curiosities into lines of conversation with God. And these days, this prayer dialogue was rapidly transforming into one of spiritual panic, begging and pleading with the God of Wonders to restore my faith in him, even just my confidence in his very existence.

Far beyond the ever-churning fountain in the back of my mind, I took every approach I could think of in prayer. As always, I would begin every morning by taking a knee before God. I would continue to pause throughout the day in my office for "prayer meetings" where just he and I were present. These were not new practices, but they were newly stepped up in their intensity as I wrestled for the renewal of my faith. I sought and petitioned and lamented.

Daily I confessed my ignorance and asked him to teach me.

Daily I confessed my arrogance and asked him to humble me.

Daily I confessed my human attraction to worldly treasures and asked him to free me.

But all to no avail as each passing month fell witness to the increasing erosion of my once-impenetrable faith.

Tormented.

That's how I felt.

Spiritually tormented.

God had promised to fill me with confident knowledge of his truth. And yet I felt more confused than ever.

God had promised to alleviate that confusion if I should only ask. And yet the more I asked of him, the more the confusion continued growing.

God had promised that since his Spirit lived within me, I would never be alone. And yet I felt more isolated and abandoned than ever before.

Got had promised that his Spirit would produce an ever-flowing fountain of new life from within. And yet I was growing numb inside. And apathetic. And like I was essentially dying from the inside out.

God had promised to never leave me hanging. And yet he seemed to have me dangled before him, laughing at my agony.

My mind knew where this was leading. In a most cyclical fashion, my condemned prayers fed into the pile of evidence that had already accumulated against God's reality. And that swelling pile would in turn feed into even-more-frantic prayers of petition.

But I couldn't give up.

He had to be there.

My entire life had been defined by him.

The absolute of my identity had been cut as a follower of Jesus.

And if God was gone, *then who was I?*

What was I?!?

Where was I?!?!?

No, *God HAD to be there.*

I wasn't yet ready to receive a godless universe.

I could NOT give up.

And the fight for my faith—the fight to reconcile my real-world experience with my faith in the existence of a god—*any god*—a god of Christian origin or *not*—was killing me.

And in the process, this fight for my faith

was

slowly
driving
me
in
s
a
n
e

One night that winter, I had planned a late night at the office, one filled with productivity and with the catching-up of projects. This was normal. I would work until around 2 a.m. and provide myself a good jump ahead. I had always loved working late into the night, all by myself in the quiet peace of an empty building and left without the distraction of appointments and staff. At least, that's what these evenings used to be.

But all of that was beginning to change.

On this particular evening, I paused my work around 10 or 11 p.m. I needed guidance on a roadblock I was up against, so I paused to ask God for his direction. And before I knew it, my entire evening was derailed in an unending quest for more of God.

It started mild yet unshakable, steadily growing in its intensity. By 1 a.m, I would find myself spread across my office floor in petition, as if I had cast myself before a king declaring my surrender to him. An emotional mess and petitioning for some respite from the spiritual agony that had been boiling just beneath the surface of each moment of every day.

God was taunting me. And I was begging to know why. With a simple word from above he could relieve my confusion and feelings of abandonment, and yet he held that word back. With the flick of a switch he could illuminate my mind to help me see what facts I was missing in my observations of the world, and yet he refused. He was taunting me.

By 2 a.m., my desperation would escalate so frantically that I'd be curled up in a writhing fetal ball, fingertips clawing at my scalp like some character from any film featuring an asylum. I begged and pleaded with God to return my sanity. I reminded him that the Bible's King Nebuchadnezzar went insane for denying God, not for clinging to him.

I would continue this for a couple more hours.

And by 4 a.m. my body would be emptied of life and breath. Eyes bloodshot and swollen. Throat dry and barbed. Body immobile. Collapsed in my chair and staring out the window into the blankness of the night. Dazed, depleted, and feeling vacant of mind, I would extend my arm toward the refrigerator with the most molasses of slow motion. I would pull out a water bottle and close the door, raise my other arm to twist off the cap, and then hold the bottle in the air in front of me. I would wonder to myself if things like water should still matter once God is gone. I would utter the words out loud, *"Probably not."* But I would bring the bottle to my lips anyway.

Then steadying my footing, I would leverage my body from its chair and fumble around for my keys. One step in front of its former, I would stumble out of my corner office, balancing myself with walls and cabinets. The work I had planned for that evening would wait until morning.

And an anesthetized shell with warzone eyes would make its way home, hoping only to find that its wife was fast asleep. Dispossessed of the ability to commit more words to air, the last thing it could afford was a live conversation with an actual person. And one with her about the chaos of its disarray, even less so.

If this evening near the end of 2010 may appear to be a proverbial rock bottom, it was the kind of rock bottom that I'd begin returning to with greater and greater frequency over the months ahead, eventually landing here on a weekly basis.

Preaching and teaching. Training teams and leading a staff. And then up all night clawing at my scalp and trying to rejuvenate my faith in an invisible god.

Welcome to the secret life of Pastor Drew.

Questions for the Dialogue

There may be much to discuss from this chapter. Here are a few questions to get us started. Feel free to create more on your own.

For Believing Christians

- Would you expect a follower of another religion to leave their religion and follow yours? If so, what would you say to them to convince them to do so? If you were born into another religion, what do you suspect would convince you to convert to Christianity? To what degree might you inadvertently hold other religions to higher standards of evidence than your own?

- If, hypothetically, you discovered a greater truth outside of Christianity, would you follow that truth or would you stick with Christianity at all costs?

- If people of other religions have a hard time making sense of their faith, should they take this as a red flag warning them against the truth of their religion? And if you ever have a hard time making sense of your faith, should it likewise be seen as a red flag?

- When was the last time you struggled to make sense of your faith? Have you ever felt like trying to make sense of your faith was driving you crazy? What are the implications here?

- Is faith best grounded in observable evidence and compelling reasons or is it best left to tradition and personal comforts? How ought we decide one over the other?

For Atheists and Skeptics

- It can be tempting to assume that religious believers don't know how to think critically, but how might their thought processes be more complex than what appearances portray?

- What assumptions might you have made at various points in your life that had to be reconciled with other information and were ultimately proven wrong? What was it that you had to reconcile and what was it like to go through that process?

- Have you ever felt confused by conflicting observations and insights? Was it ever so severe that you felt like it was almost driving you crazy? If not, can you imagine such a situation?

- When the scientific process yields conflicting results from time to time, how do we ultimately decide which way to go? How might initial assumptions influence such a process? In what ways might a religious person's initial assumptions be similar to a conflicting set of test results and in what ways are they different? And how can we come alongside religious believers to help them through the process in a way that both respects and challenges them as independent thinkers?

- What can you do to be on the lookout for others going through a crisis of faith such as is found in this chapter? And what might be the best approach to helping them navigate their way through it?

Chapter Eight

.∎∎∎..∎∎.∎∎·∎∎

As Sand Through My Fingers:
Final Attempts to Keep the Faith

If the way the last chapter ended gave you the impression that I had found my breaking point, your impression would be quite profoundly wrong. You see, as the new year was about to dawn, I was determined to employ an enhanced set of spiritual tactics in my effort to let God rebuild my faith. I was thirsting for a fresh new drink of faith and spiritual vibrancy and had come up with a plan to achieve it.

Spiritual discipline is a concept that a wide variety of religionists are familiar with. Though for many traditions this might carry dark and twisted connotations, for the evangelical Christian it is largely positive. The comparison is often made to *athletic discipline*, that is, to physical exercise. We think of "getting in shape" as a good thing and approach it in positive terms, molding our bodies into peak physical condition through the rigorous practice of exercise routines. And as such, we look forward to big-picture successes even if the particular structures and disciplines themselves aren't always enjoyable at the moment. And so for the evangelical, *spiritual discipline* is approached in much the same way, embracing the practice of concrete actions to deepen one's dependence and expectancy on God, resulting in a peak *spiritual* condition.

When evangelicals talk about *the disciplines* they're usually referring to such practices as devotional Bible reading, Bible memorization, meditation, fasting, service projects, and various kinds and formats of prayer. It can also include less common practices such as taking a day to sit in silence or to even go on a private retreat with God. At times, some will develop more personalized or even creative disciplines such as setting a timer to pause for thanksgiving every thirty minutes throughout one's day.

Now, for well over a decade I had been a man of intentional spiritual discipline. I had already incorporated everything from the list above into my regular lifestyle. Every morning I'd wake up, take a knee in prayer before my King, and ask if there was any part of my daily habit that he'd like me to sacrifice before him that day. At regular intervals I would fast from various things I enjoyed, just to prove to myself that I could live without them and to demonstrate my earnest desire for more of God, not more of coffee or wine or meat or television. And whenever a craving would arise, I'd use the opportunity to pause and pray that God would convert my appetite into a craving for more of him instead.

That is spiritual discipline.

And so in the early months of 2011, in my unending pursuit of God, I thought maybe—*just maybe*—the key to rediscovering faith could be found in stepping up my level of discipline even further. And I decided to bring the entire church along with me. I had decided to commit the months of January and February toward a church-wide campaign of spiritual renewal called "Devoted to the Divine." We would spend each week focusing on a different discipline, preaching about its usefulness, and encouraging each church member to participate in a set of individual and community activities that would enhance both our dependence upon God and our anticipation for his further work in our lives and within our church. And honestly, the series went really well as every week I heard more stories of how God's Spirit was using it to encourage and rejuvenate the lives of our people. The whole church seemed excited for where it all might lead.

And alongside the church campaign, I also spent these months diving into a fresh oasis of devotional material. I normally gravitated toward more academic types of books. I usually preferred to draw upon research materials to help me better understand the biblical text and context. And this was prioritized with the assumption that as long as I had a proper understanding of God's Word, his Spirit would feed my soul as needed. And as such, I tended to stay away from the more fluffy or self-help side of Christian reading.

But not anymore. I entered January of 2011 spiritually desperate and looking to bathe my soul in a fresh oasis of devotional reading that would affirm and replenish my faith.

And so I was now prayerfully soaking my heart and mind in the works of Oswald Chambers and A. W. Tozer. I spent every single day immersed in the classic *Book of Common Prayer* and meditating my way through the historic creeds of the ancient church. Lest these more old-school works prove too archaic, I also infused my devotional reading with the more contemporary writings of Max Lucado, Phil Yancey, and John Ortberg, along with the passionate calls of John Piper, Francis Chan, and David Platt.

I devoured Richard Foster's *Prayer: Finding the Heart's True Home*. His work overflows with powerful and inspiring stories as it introduces readers to no less than twenty-one different forms of prayer. And as you might expect, I eagerly began incorporating all twenty-one into my routine.

I also returned to the apologetic defenses. The whole point of these works is to meet nonbelievers on a logical level and reason them to belief in the Christian God. So in those months I reread C. S. Lewis, Josh McDowell, Lee Strobell, Ravi Zacharias, Tim Keller, and yes, Dinesh D'Souza. I had always detested the illogical runaround of Ray Comfort and Kirk Cameron, but I gave them another shot as well.

Anything that could even possibly light my soul aflame once more.

Absolutely anything.

But once again, I kept noticing the vastly different and even blatantly contradictory perspectives among all these authors. I had looked toward them to build up and repair my faith beyond what the Bible alone seemed competent to do, but this months-long exercise had only driven me to even greater frustration, once again emphasizing how these books ultimately formed nothing more than a collection of merely human ideas. There was no God present to authoritatively direct or unite them. They were just a group of religionists groping in the dark like the rest of us. And in the end, these readings just left me once again feeling all the more spiritually frustrated, disoriented, and without hope.

Last Straws

The common "last straw" metaphor is of a camel carrying a large pile of straw across its back. I don't know, probably tens of thousands of straws, maybe even hundreds of thousands. And more straws are being added. And as the load grows heavier and the camel more weary, he begins to buckle under pressure. Finally, one more straw is added, and it's that last straw—*as small and insignificant as it may be in and of itself*—that proves too much for the camel. And it breaks his back, crushing his existence beneath the load of individually weightless straws.

That's the common metaphor. But the one I always pictured was different. I kept thinking of a large basket *made out of* straw. And in that straw basket, I carried that which I held more dearly than anything else. The basket was my faith, and in it I held the collection of my many beloved and cherished beliefs. But the bottom of my straw basket was wearing out. Its contents weighed so heavily that its bottom grew increasingly threadbare. I struggled to hold the basket and bridge its gaps with my arms and fingers, but the individual straws were quickly giving out. Unless the basket of my faith were to find a hasty repair, it would only be a matter of time before it would all fall through the bottom.

But an even stronger image had nestled in my mind, one of a sandcastle on the shore of my soul. It was a majestic glimmering creation about to be ransacked by impending waves. Though I diligently scooped it up in my arms of rescue and ran in search of high ground, the more frantically I struggled to hold it together and the closer I buried it to my chest, the more its sand slipped through my fingers. And the more I tried to recapture its sand midair, the more quickly I lost what remained, until I held nothing more than a few once-glimmering grains. And soon even those would escape me.

At this point in my ministry, I was participating in several pastoral peer groups. Some of these were more formal and professional in nature, something of a mastermind group where we could draw from the experiences and perspectives of other pastors in an effort to do our jobs more effectively. And other groups were more along the lines of informal prayer and fellowship gatherings for pastors, providing the kind of spiritual care to one another that we were expected to provide those in our congregations.

But the group I was most excited about wedded these two concepts together. It was part of a network of pastoral peer groups put together and led by a local businessman, and my particular group was purposefully limited to participants who were male senior pastors, those charged with leading their entire organizations. Our group numbered generally around ten or so but evolved as new participants joined and others stepped away. But for the most part, it was a solid and steady group of men who were whip-smart and fully committed to each other's successes.

As someone who knew the demands of running an organization, the local businessman served as moderator, assessing group discussions from an unfiltered nonpastoral lens. His role had the benefit of suppressing the kind of competition you might otherwise see in a group of pastors, who often have a tendency to try to one-up each other in an attempt to be the *real leader* in the group. No, here all the pastors were on equal footing. I loved the setup.

We met monthly and placed one pastor "on the hot seat" in advance of each gathering. The bulk of our time would be devoted to three agenda items, which the holder of the hot seat would select in advance. He would arrive with short presentations on each of three challenges he was facing in ministry and set them before the group, asking for their experience, input, and constructive criticism. Then right there in the meeting, he would put together action steps implementing the group's feedback. The group would then follow up with him in future meetings where he would report back on progress made.

Two of these challenges were to center on the work of leading one's church, on matters such as developing a new community initiative, dealing with a troublesome staff member, or selecting a new program curriculum. Then the third and final challenge of discussion was to be a personal obstacle—since a pastor's private life *is* a professional issue. This final challenge could center on anything from one's prayer life to one's marriage. It could focus on sex addiction or substance abuse, mental health or spiritual stamina, dealing with one's parents or one's children. But whatever the topic, discussion was always intense. It was candid. It navigated through peripherals and cut right to core issues. And at times, you felt like the group's participants were openly filleting your soul right there in the conference room. But sometimes it hurts to get healthy, and the group was always generous in spirit. We were building healthier pastors with more effective ministries.

I absolutely loved my group and dove in with full force. Sitting down with these men to sharpen iron and raise the quality of our work was thrilling to me. I've always enjoyed cutting through the bullshit and engaging in honest dialogue. I thrive on fearless innovation and a push for real solutions. And I've always believed those things are best found within the community of perspectives and experiences. As I would have said back then, spirituality is inherently a group endeavor. And that that's why God gave us one another.

But on top of all this, I deeply needed some friends in my life that I could rely on and go to with life's daily problems and stresses—men I could trust. Now it's true, I kept in touch with another pastor from my days at Bethel. His name was Rob and he was absolutely amazing, the kind of guy you could share anything with. We'd get together every couple months or so and bare each other's souls to one another. He knew the full story of my wrestles with doubt and was totally supportive of me. And it was great talking with him.

But we were both busy, and I guess you can never have too much support or too many friends. So I suppose I was hoping to find that day-to-day support in these men. And who knew, maybe one day I'd even tell this group about my draw toward atheism.

Not yet, mind you.

But maybe one day.

At the January 2011 meeting, one of our friends was talking about the need for retreat every six months or so, time away at a monastery or cabin in the woods, free of distraction. He was talking about how it was part of our job to keep fresh in the faith and to regularly take time away from the demands of leading an organization, to just get away and refocus on our own personal relationships with God so that upon our return we could minister all the more effectively.

His words resonated with me. And I wondered if that's what I needed. I had been working so hard fighting to get my faith back and was completely exhausted. Physically, emotionally, and spiritually, just exhaustively depleted. But maybe getting away for a couple days to just sit in silence before God is what I needed. Less fighting, more sitting. I wondered if God was perhaps speaking to me through my friend's words, telling me that this would be the turning point.

So I selected this quiet little monastic center a couple hours south of Chicago, one run by a Catholic sisterhood. The plan was to spend two full days in one of their rustic hermitages. No electricity. No noise. No other people. Just me and the Spirit of God in the woods alone. It would be marvelous. And I really believed it would be.

I booked my date and drew a large red circle on my calendar.

Despite all my increased efforts, I was feeling as insane as ever. The midnight office hijackings of torture that I described earlier now occurred on almost a weekly basis. I was growing more crazed by the day. I felt like the spider on Jonathan Edwards' web with God holding me over a fire laughing at my agony.

Or maybe he was just testing my faith.

And maybe it was at the retreat that he would reveal himself once more.

There the darkness would be defeated once and for all.

Just like in the fairytales.

God, I needed this retreat.

But the retreat never happened. After weeks of planning and the elevation of expectations, I faced a minor family emergency the morning I was set to leave for the retreat. I spent a couple hours trying to work the logistics so I could keep my booking at the monastery. But to no avail.

The God who could hold back all the family emergencies covering the entire globe with the snap of a personified finger had decided not to. He had cancelled our meeting.

I was devastated.

I was shocked to silence.

I was overcome with disbelief.

But mostly, I was just seething. I was resentful and bitter. I was mad as hell.

I was mad as hell at God.

I yelled at him. I accused God of leading me on, of promising me a respite oasis that he knew I desperately needed, only to intentionally leave me hanging. I threatened him that if he really wanted to build my faith and affirm in me that he really was real, that this probably wasn't the best way to go about it. I lashed out that for a god claiming to be so all-powerful and full of control, you'd think he could do a better job keeping his shit together.

And then the back corners of my mind reminded me.

It's possible that God had nothing to do with the retreat's demise. That for all my fighting to force myself to believe and pretend that there was a god out there to talk to and to depend upon and to try to trust in, maybe it's time to face reality. Maybe it's time for me to end all the self-induced insanity and the torment of trying to make myself make something irrational feel rational. Maybe it's time for me to finally face the reality, the reality that God just isn't real.

The Final Straw That Sparked a Fire

In the brief handful of weeks that followed, I felt my faith being eaten alive by doubt. And for the first time, prayer itself seemed to damage my faith. Even just a few weeks earlier, I could pray something simple like, *"God if you're there, please . . ."* and I could rest for at least a couple hours in the possibility. But not anymore. Every moment of prayer had now grown anxious, bitter, and restive.

And now in the month of March any fragments of faith that had remained on life support would now die away into a complete absence of God whatsoever. Just the complete vacancy of my soul. Casting my tireless efforts across the previous months, I'd now realized I had been working double time just to manufacture a spiritual dialogue with God that left me physically exhausted and spiritually confused. I'd been toiling away at those disciplines in order to breathe some semblance of fresh air into the lungs of my soul—like the despondent one who slaps himself just to feel the pain that tells him he's still alive. But I was the one doing all the work, not God. I was the industrialist. And each time I'd pause the work for a moment, all sense of divine presence would immediately disappear.

Now, I hadn't planned on bringing any of this up with the professional peer groups I was involved with. They were great guys, but I wasn't sure I could really trust them with something so, well, *sensitive*. But it had just so happened that March was my month to return to that damned hot seat.

So a week in advance of the meeting and just one week following my cancelled retreat, I had a phone conference with the group moderator to go over my three agenda items. For my two organizational matters, I had settled quite easily on the need to boost church revenue and on my development plan for our church's elder council.

But for the third agenda item, which had to be more personal in nature, I was struggling. There was so much I *wanted* to say and yet so little felt *safe* to say. But I thought there might still be something I could glean from what were becoming my last ditch efforts to keep the faith. So in a final act of desperation, clinging to those final shards, I planned to present my devotional plan and ask the group for tips on what they've found helpful in their own spiritual formation. This would allow me to gain insight on holding my faith together without actually confessing to them how it was falling apart.

That morning, we met together as planned. Not everyone was able to make it that day, so I honestly can't say exactly who was there and who was not. But I want to say eight of us joined together in anticipation of another great session.

Breakfast and small talk, check.

Church finances, check.

Leadership development, check.

So as I approached my hot seat's final agenda item, everything was running smoothly and as expected. I began by reading through the six-point overview I had put together, describing my current practices involving prayer, meditation, fasting, etc. I then invited the group's feedback, saying that I was genuinely curious what habits they had found helpful in their own devotional lives.

There was a jump to diagnose the reason why I wanted to upgrade my spiritual formation in the first place. All I wanted was specific ideas from their own lives, yet no one seemed willing to share their own personal practices.

How's that for avoiding the question? I wondered.

Conversation quickly focused on the immensity of my schedule and workload. I needed to allow time for rest and balance, I was told. From there, I was asked what *fears* led me to be such a workaholic. Now, all of this might make for a great conversation, even critical points for self-examination, but it was a bit off topic from what I really wanted help with. Or at least *I* thought it was.

And then I began to feel uncomfortable with where the discussion was turning. All this talk of *fears* and *underlying issues*, I began feeling a little flustered and exposed and without escape. *No wonder they called it the hot seat!*

They kept pressing. I kept deflecting.

Until eventually I began to wonder if I should just come clean with what was bothering me. Just let it all out, so we could deal with the real issue at hand. *Maybe some good would come out on the other end? Healing even?* And yet, I wasn't sure. It's never good to change your mind on something important in the heat of the moment, and I had previously decided not to tell them about my growing disbelief.

And then.

And then the group moderator said he could tell something was bothering me, and he asked what it was. *What's the real issue here?* he pushed. He was a robust man of great physical size, and when passionate, he seemed angry. Certainly forceful. And now he seemed forcefully angry as he pushed me.

What's the real issue here?

We can't deal with it until it's on the table!

And just like that, I lost all ability or even desire to contain or conceal it further. Every ounce of strength had been required to not get their help and counsel on my doubts, and now I had eight pastors plus my moderator all staring me down, asking about my fears and my anxieties and what keeps me up at night and what petitions dominate my prayer life, and I had no idea what to say next. They just kept looking at me, shooting off more and more questions born in the pit of the earth and awaiting my reply.

So I did it.

I did what I swore to myself that I wouldn't do.

I let it out.

I spilled the beans.

Well, the sand, really. I spilled the cascading sand of my half-twitching faith all out on the table.

Then I took a deep breath. And with the floodgates of my eyes stretched to capacity, I told them that I was entrenched in the greatest battle of faith I had ever seen. *My faith is being consumed by doubts, overtaken,* I told them. *Eaten from the inside out.* I said that I had been trying to just pray and trust God but that it seemed the more I prayed and cried out to him, the worse it grew. I told them I could barely read my Bible without seeing an unending line of holes and problems. I told them I desperately wanted to have my old level of belief back, that I loved my faith and wanted God to be real, but that I honestly wasn't sure if I even believed anymore. *As if sand spilling through my fingers,* I told them, *the harder I worked to keep my faith held tightly, the more elusive it had become.*

My frantic confession probably lasted three or four minutes, and then I paused.

I really didn't know what to expect as a response, but although I realized I might possibly be condemned on the spot—especially since most of the pastors were measurably more conservative than I was and even downright fundamentalist, I was nonetheless hopeful for some consolation and wisdom to move me forward in retaking my faith. Maybe someone would even offer to meet with me on a regular basis, to help bind my wounds and shoulder a broken brother's burden. If on the other side of this torturous experience, I discovered a brother who had been here before and would be willing to start meeting with me to mentor me back to full and faithful health, well then it would have all been worth it.

But instead I received an eternal reverberation of silence and blank stares.

I had never seen such a lack of response from the group on any discussion topic, neither before my confession nor after it. Always overflowing with ideas while members compete for speaking time, this group of preachers and teachers now sat oddly and inexplicably inaudible. Literally beginning to shake in disbelief, I scanned the table as each member suddenly found themselves at a loss of speech, eyebrows crumpled and without a word of dictum or gloss. A few looked nervous. Two sets of eyes blinked. One, a second time. And that was it.

Perpetual silence . . .

Or at least for a minute or two

And then, at last, one of them *finally* spoke up, one of the older and more old-school pastors. I don't recall his exact words but I will never misplace their effect. He tried to comfort me, I guess. Apparently he was trying to be empathetic and identify with my pain while also sobering me up to the unpleasant reality of Christian faith. He said that he understood my doubts because he had felt them too. Everyone at that table, he assured me, had suffered from those very same doubts. *But*, he said, *we are pastors—what are we supposed to do? Stop pastoring? Just quit and walk away because our faith feels threatened?*

Everyone was nodding in agreement. They too knew the pain of doubt.

"But," I struggled to clarify, "these are not mere everyday doubts. I've seen those from time to time and throughout the years. But that's not what this is. I am being *overwhelmed* by my doubts. My faith is being *consumed* by doubts, completely overtaken. The depth of my doubt is so fundamental, I'm not even sure I believe in the existence of God anymore! My faith is on the brink of complete and total collapse and I don't know what to do!"

This time, I was immediately offered a cheap "Hang in there brother" and a nodding of the head. I think he also put his hand on my shoulder. So there's that.

Then more silence.

A whole room full of pastors avoiding eye contact. Zombie stares into outer space and nervous awkward twitching.

Then the moderator, the businessman who was the only nonpastor in the room, offered the only real response. He normally wasn't one to offer advice or counsel. That's what the pastors were for. He was to simply protect from clerical dictators and to defeat long-winded sermonettes. But here, in this situation, someone needed to move the conversation forward. And he seemed both mystified and terribly frustrated that others weren't saying more. He had tried to contain himself but could do so no more. So he offered his perspective.

He said that it seemed clear to him that I had been reading too many liberal books, too much secular atheistic garbage. That it had infected my thinking and clouded my spiritual discernment. He advised that I simply get back to the Word of God. Marinate my soul in the Bible and some good devotional literature. It was time to reject Satan, he exhorted me. Time to come clean and simply sit at the feet of Jesus.

As if he had any idea . . .

Yet, I couldn't blame him for thinking that way. He was never told of endless prayers that extended hours past midnight. He had no idea what my reading list was, or that up until this point I had never read even a single work of liberal theology, much less one promoting atheism. He had no idea how saturated my soul was in good Jesus-loving literature. He hadn't heard the begging and pleading or seen my eyes repeatedly swollen with longing for more of my Heavenly Father. He just simply had no idea.

But it is interesting nonetheless, that the only nonpastor in the room is the one who attempted even the slightest stroke of real counsel, be it critical or constructive. He was the only one that saw something troubling with my situation. The only one vocally disturbed, refusing to nod in affirmation. It is interesting indeed that all the pastors in the room sat with slow-motion head nods of hushed identification while the only pastor to speak proclaimed on their behalf that their own doubts were just as grievous as mine.

I left the meeting with my faith in greater tatters than before. As I said earlier, I'm not sure what the pastor's exact words were and I certainly do not intend to put words in his mouth. But what it felt like to me is that every one of those pastors doubted the very existence of God as much as I did, that every one of them had questions as serious as mine about the Bible's credibility, and that every single one of them had come to the resignation that their faith was not all they had thought it to be when they had first entered ministry.

In fact, it even sounded like my dear friend was suggesting that the only reason they remained in ministry was because their graduate degrees and professional experience was good for little else. It almost sounded as if he said, *What do you expect us to do? Wait on tables the rest of our lives??? So yes, we practice a faith we don't believe and preach doctrines that fail to convince us. Because after all and at the end of the day, we've got bills to pay and mouths to feed.*

I prayed to God that I was being overly sensitive and that I simply misunderstood his words. But then again, that really was what it sounded like.

And when I wanted to update the group on my faith situation at the next month's meeting, I was bypassed without comment. Sharing updates was the critical closing segment of each meeting. We called this the "round table," and we'd each go around the room, taking turns getting the group up to speed on previous commitments and firing off questions to keep one another on target. As with the hot seat segment, so was the round table likewise relentless. Nothing could slip by as the group would be asking you about your situation for months on end.

But not this. Not with my faith situation. When I tried updating the group at that April meeting, it was once again a room of awkward twitches. I was nearly cut off midsentence as time constraints demanded we kept moving forward.

And it was never brought up again.

I saw most of these men on a regular basis, even weekly at times. Not a single one of them ever brought it up to me again. Never asked about it. Never inquired. It was like it had been wiped clean from the desktop of each one's mind.

But back to the day of the March meeting.

I left that meeting in a state of crisis.

I wasn't sure to what degree my peer group represented the remainder of the Christian church. If anything, due to their conservative Christian theology, I had assumed the quality of their faith would be stronger than that of your average clergyperson. But then again, maybe I was just biased. I was beginning to wonder if the hard honest truth was that those least likely to truly believe in the Christian god were those who had studied him and sought after him most diligently. In other words, pastors. Maybe you just can't see the imperfections until you're close enough to kiss without the makeup on.

It's interesting that this is where my thoughts had taken me that afternoon. It would be just a couple weeks after this that something known as The Clergy Project would be launched, providing a private online community of support and encouragement to those religious professionals who no longer held supernatural beliefs. But I knew nothing of this group back then. And it wouldn't be for another three years until I would even hear of this wonderful little community. *More on this later . . .*

But I left that meeting completely debilitated, and I had reached my breaking point. It was the final straw. A straw that caught fire and torched the whole basket beyond repair. For all practical purposes, you can count March 2, 2011, as the day my faith died. I suppose it wasn't quite that clean-cut, but I left that meeting feeling as if I had now passed an absolutely God-forsaken point of no return. The clock had struck midnight and the hope of resurrection was empty.

Questions for the Dialogue

Everyone's story is unique, but we all face similar questions. Let's take some time to think through the bigger picture of the role doubt plays in all our lives.

For Everyone

- Is it surprising to see the struggle between faith and doubt that can sometimes brew beneath the surface? How might this more fully inform our assumptions about believers who appear confident on the outside?

- Have any of your own struggles sometimes mirrored those in this chapter? Were they religious in nature or of another variety?

- What do you make of the pastoral peer group and their response when confronted with a fellow pastor's disbelief? To what extent might this indicate their own level of personal doubts? Or is there another way to interpret their response? To what degree might this group be representative of the whole of Christian clergy? And to what point representative of the whole of all world religions? What might be some further implications here?

For Believing Christians

- What's the difference between truly believing something and living life as if you believe? To what extent might the latter itself serve as an act of faith? How might these distinctions be important?

- What kind of situation in life do you think would be the hardest on your faith? What kind of support system do you think would help you make it through with your faith intact? And what would you then do if that support system failed you?

- In this pastor's efforts to do everything possible to regain his faith, what might he have missed? Is there anything he could have done differently or more effectively? If in a similar situation, how would you have handled it?

- If you genuinely wanted to believe in something that all the evidence seemed stacked against, how long would it take before you gave up and quit trying? How long do you think someone should keep trying to believe in God before they let go and quit trying to force themselves to believe?

- Is it possible to simply will yourself to believe in something you don't believe in? If someone told you that you had to honestly and sincerely believe in the existence of Santa Claus, could you? What about the existence of little green men living on the moon? Or what about another god like Zeus or Ganesha or the god of Islam? Are these comparisons fair? Why or why not?

For Atheists and Skeptics

- Sometimes the struggle a believer faces when giving up their faith in God can be quite intense. As you consider their level of struggle, how might some of them find the struggle itself unexpected? What situations might make it easier for them to walk away from belief in a god? What situations might make it more difficult?

- Consider the various ways a nonbeliever could respond toward someone who is actively clinging to their faith in God. What might be the short-term effects of these various responses? What about the long-term effects? What might be the best approach to take with an acquaintance who seems determined in their faith? What about with a close friend?

Chapter Nine

"What Now?":
Resigning from the Ministry and Other Next Steps

As the spring months bled into the summer it grew increasingly clear that I had to seriously consider leaving the pastorate. It would still be more than a year before I could comfortably think of myself as an atheist, but I knew that if something didn't change quickly, that's the direction I was headed in. *And God, did I hope he might still bring my faith back!*

But it seemed that maybe if I just got away from the whole rat race, away from the demands of caring for everyone else's souls twenty-four seven, away from their nonstop crises at all hours day or night, away from the demands of leading an entire organization—that maybe if I could break away from it all, I would find a space there to care for my own needs more fully. And maybe in that space I would discover a truth bigger than anything I had previously seen. It had become clear at this point that a god as conceived in the Christian Bible was simply impossible. But maybe there was something else out there. Maybe a Christian-ish god that kind of looked similar but wasn't bound to a flawed and ancient text. Maybe it was something completely different. Maybe. Just maybe.

But then I'd look around and wonder if there were any questions that weren't satisfied with a completely naturalistic worldview. Again if I'd known nothing of religion, was there anything in the world—*or anything in my experience of the world*—that would naturally point me toward belief in any type of godlike being?

Any compelling reason to suggest another layer of reality that lies beyond this natural one? Again, it seemed clear to me that there was not.

But in it all, one thing was clear. I couldn't be a pastor anymore. For one of two reasons—*or maybe it was really just one reason with two sides*. Either way, here's how my thinking went: if Christianity was myth, I simply could not allow myself to knowingly perpetuate false truths, and if God was not real, I could not condemn people to an imaginary hell and a life of psychological torment just to fulfill a career. I just couldn't. I had to reject this as a possible pathway. But on the other hand, if there *really was* some sort of god out there, I had clearly lost all ability to discern such truths. And the dear, sweet people of my church, they deserved someone who could. So either Christian ministry was unfit for this world or I was unfit for Christian ministry. But either way, I had to transition out.

But to what?

Church work was all I had ever really wanted to do. If not as a pastor, certainly in roles connected to the big-picture work of the global church. The very center of how I had always envisioned myself was as a pastor first-and-foremost with anything that might follow building off of it. Never before had I even considered a move cultivated from any other foundation than this.

Until now.

I'm often asked a question that is often asked of all deconverted pastors. Everyone wants to know how my ministry practices may have evolved through this process. *How did my preaching change? Did I start emphasizing a different set of Bible verses? Did I stop preaching from the Bible altogether?* Alternatively, sometimes instead of preaching more liberal doctrine or politics, closeted disbelievers might actually take on a more *fundamentalist* message in order to prevent getting caught. *So in what direction did my preaching evolve? How did my pastoral counseling change? Did I advise my congregation differently in their personal lives? Did I stop praying with people who came to me for help?*

The short answer is *no*.

No, in that there weren't any outward changes. I continued everything just as I always had right up to the very end.

See, it was always my view that pastors must keep personal matters out of the way when doing their work. And *this* was a personal matter. It was not to affect how I did my job. That's called leadership. I had worked according to a preaching and teaching schedule designed to systematically cover every verse in the Bible, and I continued along that line. Even the tough stuff. My philosophy of preaching made this easy, however. I had never been the kind of pastor who claimed to have all the answers. I would point to a biblical or theological conundrum and simply say, *Well, everybody, I'm honestly not sure what to do with this verse. But here are the options. And I'm confident that as long as we trust in God, he will lead our thinking as he wants it to go.* So that style of openness was easier to continue than a more dogmatic doctrinal approach. But I never stopped telling my congregation to trust in God. He was the source of truth.

And I was preaching to myself as much as I was to them.

Still grasping to hold my own faith together, the last thing I wanted to do to my church was lead them away from belief. If back then I was where I am today, I would have worked to help them be more critical of their beliefs. I would have worked to steer the entire church in a more agnostic or even atheistic direction. But I wasn't there back then. I still desperately wanted my beliefs back. And I wanted to protect theirs at all costs.

Which meant I needed to remove myself.

Career Options for the Deconverting Pastor

I had already put myself through college and grad school waiting on tables. And everything else I had ever done beyond that was all church work. Sure, I had also bagged groceries while I was in high school. And I had spent a summer working for my dad at his industrial plant. And I suppose if we go back even further to when I was a twelve-year-old kid, it's true I had also spent a couple summers picking rock for a local farmer.

But everything else I had ever done professionally was bound up in church work. My bachelor's degree was in pastoral studies. My graduate degree was a Master of Divinity in pastoral ministry. These don't exactly translate well into a secular career. And back then I had absolutely no idea that such a translation was even possible.

My skills weren't much more marketable than my education. At least not anything I was able to see at the time. I was an expert in biblical research and communication. And that was about it.

But I didn't really even know anything about the more technical side of nonprofit leadership, in terms of document filings or grant writing or taxes. I had a team of people who knew all about those kinds of things. I delegated it all to them and they told me what I needed to know, when I needed to know it.

I didn't really know anything about building computers or fixing them. Neither did I know anything about online networks and such. I delegated that stuff out to the computer guys. For as much as I was always online and blogging and making sure our church's website was flashy and hip and updated with current information, I didn't have a clue how to code or use a lot of fancy programs.

I had never had a trade. I wasn't a carpenter. I knew nothing of cars.

I had always been trained that as pastors, we simply needed to know God and his Word and that he would take care of the rest. No need for any other training. Lead his people to trust in God, and God will lead in all other facets of life.

I was pretty damn good at leading a team, at group dynamics, at pulling and utilizing the best in people, of putting them in just the right place and motivating them toward greatness. These are things that will make you a great leader. And when your technical expertise is biblical research, education, and social interaction, you'll be a great *church* leader.

But take away the church part and you're just a guy who's good with people but lacks any technical expertise in anything of value.

Not a résumé to gain much attention.

And I couldn't leave the church without something solid. Not only was my family of four's health insurance tied to my work at the church, but so too was our housing. We lived on church property and in one of its houses. Keep in mind this had been a small church about to shutter its doors when I arrived, but it had a large campus with several buildings from back in the good old days. And a great way for a small church to compensate a pastor is through housing rather than through additional salary. But the bottom line, I wouldn't just need a new job; I'd also need new housing. And the car I drove was also owned by the church. Each of these layers would need to be considered and addressed before I could just go running off without a game plan.

I considered staying.

I considered staying on at the church. I did love the work, and I also loved the people. They loved me and never treated my wife and daughters as anything less than true family. What if I just stayed on and played the charade? Just as I might with any other soulless job that paid the bills. Play the role and sell the product regardless of whether I personally believed in it or not.

But as I said earlier, I just couldn't do that. I had always been a transparent, what-you-see-is-what-you-get kind of leader, and I couldn't change that now.

So yes, I considered staying and honestly leading West Hills in whatever direction the truth should seem to me to point, even if that truth pointed beyond—*or even in opposition to*—Christianity. But though the church was fairly progressive by evangelical standards, I really didn't think there was any way they'd follow such a course. A progressive reading of the inerrant Bible was one thing, but ditching inerrancy altogether and effectively convincing them to embrace a Bibleless Christianity was on an entirely other level.

And honestly, I wasn't so sure I was up for the job of taking them there anyway.

Mostly I was just exhausted from the battle over my own soul. And I looked forward to something new. Something where I could just zone out and drift a little. Or at least not have to worry about leading an entire organization. Just punching a clock sounded fantastic.

Ultimately, over the course of the next four or five months, I decided to pursue a PhD. I leaned toward theology, since it would build easily on the degrees I had already earned. But before we get too far with more career stuff, there was something else my growing disbelief demanded of me.

Telling my wife.

A Most Uninviting Conversation

Surely you've noticed by now that I haven't said much about my marriage or family life. But it would be a mistake to assume this means they weren't important to me or that I didn't play an active role in the home. I loved my family dearly, and it was a source of joy that often kept me healthy, strong, and at least halfway sane throughout the turbulence.

As you may remember, my wife's name was Justina. I talked about her a fair amount at the beginning of my little story. I described how I led her to put her faith in Jesus while we were both in high school. And now because of this, we always carried this unfortunate dynamic where she implicitly viewed me as her spiritual father. Put on top of this the fact that I was also her pastor through much of our marriage, and well, let's just say this situation might have produced some distressing and harmful effects on her ability to truly see herself as her own person and as my equal.

My own views on what conservative Christians commonly refer to as "marriage roles" were notably more progressive and egalitarian than what you'd typically expect of fundamentalist or evangelical circles. As a pastor, I did not believe in or teach traditional gender roles and continually presented marriage as a true partnership between equals. In fact, while serving in my first church as a staff pastor, I was even instructed by the senior pastor that I had gone too far in equating men and women and that I needed to make my Sunday morning preaching more traditional in this area.

So as I had seen it, Justina and I were coleaders in our home, and I had no more veto power within our family than she did. She spoke her mind freely. And actually, I really loved it when she disagreed with me. I believed our decisions were of a higher quality when we both entered into dialogue from different perspectives and were forced to negotiate. But beyond that, I wanted her—*just like I wanted everyone*—to be empowered to think for herself, and it horrified me that anyone—*but especially that she*—would ever default to my perspective on anything just because I was a pastor.

But nonetheless, maybe because I was a trained minister, maybe because of my confident personality, maybe because I might sometimes be kind of good at using words, she seemed to rely heavily on my perspective in shaping her own.

So telling her about my atheism terrified me.

It terrified me, mind you, because I still wanted my belief back. And the last thing I wanted to do was be the instigator in derailing anyone else's belief in God. *Especially hers.*

But a conversation had to take place nonetheless. Especially since I was thinking I might need to leave the pastorate. So we went for a walk one day in March, shortly after my confession to the pastors group. It was a long walk. And there I began broaching the subject of all that was churning just beneath the surface.

She had known something was going on. We'd always been very close and told each other everything. She'd known there was stuff I must have been wrestling through, but she'd also trusted I'd work my way through whatever it was and that I'd come to her if I'd ever need to.

And now I needed to.

So on the walk I explained that I was having doubts and that those doubts cut as deep as to the very existence of God himself. Honestly, I don't think she was surprised at all by the presence of my doubts. Our church community spoke often about the powerful role doubts can play in forging a stronger and more vibrant faith. We actually saw doubt as a healthy part of belief. So, no, she wasn't surprised by the presence of my doubts. Even doubts about the existence of God.

But what may have surprised her more was that the doubts had apparently won. And, as I went on to explain further, that the doubts were moving me to consider a career change.

She asked for more information. She wanted to know just what the hell had happened. What had I seen or heard or felt or studied that had caused me to completely lose my shit. She wanted me to walk her though the long line of everything that had brought me to this place. But I refused. In a nice way, of course. I told her my fear that if I shared everything with her, her faith might be killed off just as mine had been.

It took her a moment to digest my reasoning, but once she did, she understood.

And as much as it killed her not knowing all that I had seen and thought, she seemed to appreciate my unwillingness to immediately dump everything on her right away.

So during our conversation on the walk that day, I gave her some extremely vague examples of the kind of Bible contradictions that I had noticed years back. I told her of my months of prayers asking God to revitalize my faith—and that those prayers had gone unanswered. I told her that though I had fought to keep manufacturing some shred of faith, it was now hard to imagine any sort of all-powerful-and-all-loving supernatural being out there, willfully ignoring all my pleas for revival. I kept the story quite brief and the details generalized but said just enough to give her the parameters of what we were dealing with here.

Through it all, I don't ever remember her getting angry. Maybe a little frustrated. Certainly pained. Definitely confused. And it opened up a whole arena of personal searching in her own journey. But she never appeared angry with me.

And she never denied the reality I was facing. She never told me I didn't know what I was talking about. Never succumbed to what so many others have done in telling the newly deconverted that they're just overworked or depressed or burnt-out, and that once they get some rest, faith will return. She never said any of that. She knew better. And she trusted me.

And we moved forward together.

And that July, while on the way back from a Texas road trip, we determined that the need to move was inevitable. We planned what the upcoming months would look like as I began taking steps toward resignation. We talked of the future. And we dreamed of days when lack of belief wouldn't be the detrimental thing it currently seemed to be. As we discussed the future and an end to ministry, the air reverberated with a nervous breath that was nonetheless refreshing and filled with hope.

Resigning from the Ministry

So what is the final honorable act of a pastor who no longer believes what he preaches? Resignation. Or at least that's how I reasoned it.

And since teaching had long been the part of pastoral ministry that most excited me, I was looking forward to pursuing a PhD and a career in postgraduate education. Or something like that. First I needed to get the PhD and then we'd go from there.

But before I could pursue a PhD, I first needed additional study. Since the Master of Divinity is a three-year professional degree, you can't build a *research* doctorate on top of it. I'd therefore need to take one additional year of study to convert the MDiv into a four-year research master's degree called a Master of Theology. Then on top of *this*, the PhD would fit nicely. The idea was to pursue this ThM at an evangelical school and to then seek a more liberal seminary for the doctorate.

But some have wondered why on earth I'd want to leave the church only to gain two more theology degrees. They've asked why I'd still want to remain in the business of "God stuff" even as I was in the midst of becoming an atheist. But see, that's just it. I was still *in the process* of becoming an atheist. I was still in love with the *idea* of God. And I wanted to continue my pursuit of him and his truth. And in a way, I was leaving the ministry in order to create more space where I could truly follow whatever path that pursuit should lead, no matter how liberal or nonbiblical or even explicitly non-Christian a direction it should take me down.

And I still loved religion. To this day, I love reading and studying about world religions. I find them absolutely fascinating even as I find all of supernatural beliefs inherently flawed. So the idea of studying world religion and theology sounded more than exciting.

But in terms of career, being a professor sounded like the ideal vocation. Teaching was always the aspect of pastoral ministry that I most enjoyed. I could go on and on about learning styles and pedagogical methodologies for hours on end. Writing curriculum was fun. And some in the church had nicknamed me Professor Drew while college kids told me they'd pay more attention at university if I were the one teaching their classes.

So that fall I visited Trinity Evangelical Divinity School, otherwise known as TEDS. I applied to their ThM program, hoping to begin with the Fall 2012 semester. And to my delight I was accepted and awarded their Christian Leadership scholarship. I also began campus visits for the PhD as well. It was a thrilling time. I had always loved being a student and had secretly longed for more classroom hours. And now here was my opportunity. I was ecstatic.

But I also had a family of four to provide for.

Justina was just finishing her associate's degree in sign-language interpreting, but we couldn't depend on her to single-handedly pay all the bills while I hit the library every day. In order for any of this to work out, the undisputable key ingredient was that I had to find dependable secular employment before I could announce my resignation.

Hmmm . . .

I hadn't yet learned how to translate my arsenal of pastoral leadership skills into something that piqued the interest of secular headhunters. And as a result, every single résumé I sent out, each inquiry I placed to open positions in all corners of the nonprofit world, was met with rejection—*or no response at all.*

I was stuck.

And so it became clear rather quickly that my greatest opportunity would be found in approaching the downtown Chicago steakhouse where I had waited on tables for a couple years during seminary. It had been a great job with an amazing company. And what I had made in tips as a server was nearly triple what I later made as a pastor. I also knew that they'd likely be responsive since this was the same company that had offered me a management spot when I was preparing to head into full-time ministry. And just before I had left the company a friend of mine had been promoted as the new general manager. Upon my departure, he told me that should I ever be in need a job, he'd love to have me back.

So that December I called up my general-manager friend.

And I told him I needed that job.

He invited me to come in and sit down with him. And there I asked if he might have a serving position available for me in the months ahead. I explained a little of my situation and told him that once I resigned from ministry I would want to work with the board of elders on an appropriate transition. I had no interest in simply "peacing out" on this fine church with a quick two-weeks notice. I was not simply an employee. I was their leader and I needed to make sure I left them in good hands. So I told my friend that I couldn't even be sure what month I would be available, but that I wanted to get a sense of whether he might have something for me once the time arises.

And since the steakhouse only employed full-time servers back then, I also made clear that I had no intention of staying at the restaurant beyond the summer. I just wanted to generate some extra cash and pay down my credit cards before I went back to school in the fall, when I'd look for a more low-key job that would allow me to devote the needed time to my new studies.

I had feared I'd placed so many qualifiers on this job, there's no way it could happen. But my friend was immediately accommodating. He told me he'd love to have me back as a server and even began dreaming up other opportunities, should I decide to stay with the company longer term. He also told me not to worry about timing. He said I could start whenever I wanted, even if we were in the dead of a slow season. Just call him up, and I could start the following week.

So I guess you could say that that went well.

And now everything was coming together.

Educational plan, check.

Secular employment, check.

Justina was researching new school districts for the kids.

We were exploring housing options.

And now it was time to talk with West Hills Church.

But what exactly would I tell them?

The truth of course. Well, the truth minus anything about my doubts. Keep in mind again that the last thing I wanted to do was damage anyone else's faith—*have I reiterated this enough yet?*

At this point I was also still praying on a fairly regular basis. They were these just-in-case prayers, saying things like, *God, if you're out there, I just want you to know that I still wish you were real.* And I'd invite him to correct any of my flawed thinking. I never stopped inviting the Master of my mind to give me back my belief.

I also regularly asked him to correct the plan of my new career path. I'd invite him to stop me if he didn't want me to leave the church. I'd ask him to change my mind if he didn't want me to pursue a PhD or a career in postgraduate education. And I told him that I'd logically interpret any *silence* as approval of the plans I'd set before him and that in such a case I'd keep moving full-speed ahead.

And, well, at no point did God ever seem to try to stop me. He never corrected any potentially flawed thinking. So full-speed ahead I charged.

And that's what I told the church.

I met with the West Hills elder council at the beginning of January 2012. They sat there in total disbelief as I shared how over the course of that year I had been overwhelmed with an unshakable sense that my time at West Hills was coming to an end, that I felt I was being called into a teaching role, and that my repeated prayers had resulted in nothing short of absolute confirmation. This was not an easy meeting. Tears everywhere. We had so much love for one another. And it was a shock. Things were going so well at the church. We were on track and growing. New and fresh ideas continued to surge. And yet we now found ourselves at this unexpected crossroads. Sometimes change is inevitable.

After calling in the big dogs and meeting with our church network's regional leadership at Converge Mid-America, a plan was put together for my outbound transition. Normally, it's best to move exiting pastors out as quickly as possible once the news is made public. Keeps the people from feeling stuck. Keeps the organization moving forward. But in our church's particular situation, regional leadership suggested we do something a little different. A plan was put together to keep me through a six-month transition where I would essentially serve as my own part-time interim pastor as I'd help the elder council find just the right replacement and ensure a smooth movement toward the next guy.

This was hardly what I had wanted. And suddenly, that two-weeks notice and peace-out goodbye sounded monumentally better. I was dying for a respite of sanity. But more than anything, I wanted to leave the church in a good spot. And if my sticking around would leave them healthier, that was my utmost concern.

On January 29, 2012, I announced my resignation to the congregation. We talked of how sometimes life shifts before our feet and of how we will do best to be agile. We talked of how sometimes the truth leads in unexpected directions and of how we must always be willing to follow its lead—of how we must always be willing to follow where God should lead each of us as individuals. And then I spoke of how over the last year, I'd grown unsettled by an inner pull telling me I needed to change course. I told them I had labored in prayer for months on end over the decision, but that at the end of the day, God was leading me away from West Hills. He was leading me to a teaching career, beginning with the pursuit of a ThM and PhD.

An endless line of tear-filled hugs followed. I stayed on with full pastoral duties through the end of February, making all the necessary preparations so that the office could keep running without me. And then I picked up that job at the steakhouse while continuing to preach every Sunday, meet as needed with the elder council to assist with the pastoral search, and do any crisis intervention among the congregation.

Then on July 28, 2012, I preached my final sermon. After six months of transitional messages, this was a simple farewell. I took time to recount favorite memories and highlights from the past four years and delivered a simple meditation on the final words of Second Corinthians 13, which begins, "Finally brothers, goodbye." The congregation then began passing microphones as volunteers and community members shared how much Justina and I had meant to them and how God had used us to bring healing and joy to their lives. Spilling to nearly thirty minutes of stories and testimonies, we then moved to an outdoor barbeque and an afternoon of lawn games. We were a true community. And I'm not sure my love for them will ever fade. I'm not sure I'd want it to.

And then on July 29, 2012, I woke up for the first time in well over a decade as a nonpastor. Everything I had ever been was now over.

Questions for the Dialogue

When deconverted religious leaders exit ministry, the way in which they do so often comes under heavy scrutiny from all sides. Let's think through all the elements involved.

For Everyone

- Of the various concerns that often play a role in a pastor's transition out of ministry, which needs do you think should take priority in determining the method and timing?
  - Financial needs
  - Career needs
  - Educational needs
  - Housing needs
  - Family needs
  - Emotional/mental/spiritual needs
  - Church needs
  - Congregational needs
  - Truth-telling needs
  - Other :

- If a pastor has a family with young children, does this change the situation? Should the pastor think of family first and secure a replacement income before leaving the ministry, no matter how long that might take, or does the pastor have a duty to be honest with the church and congregation no matter the consequences?

For Believing Christians

- Unbelieving pastors are often criticized for not immediately sharing their doubts with the church. At what point would it be most appropriate for such a pastor to do so? Since virtually all pastors admit to having occasional doubts, would you want to know every time they have a moment of second guessing or only if their doubts were a bit more substantial? Would you want to know if doubts persist for a month? A year? And what level of doubts? Are they allowed to always kind of wonder as long as they keep it held together, or as long as they keep trying to believe, or do you want to know those details as well? What are the dividing lines? And is it possible that the issues are not as clear-cut as we would sometimes like to make them out to be?

- If a great pastor who had significantly shaped your faith came out publicly as an atheist during a Sunday morning service, what effect do you think that would have on you? Would you prefer such a pastor simply resign and leave quietly? Would you want to know about the pastor's doubts or would you prefer to have that information kept from you? Why?

- If pastors started getting up and confessing doubts more regularly, what would be the impact on the church?

- Is it fair for a pastor to hold back information in an attempt to protect or shield the congregation from something that could damage the faith of its members? Is this best viewed as an act of greater integrity or less? Or is it best assessed on a case-by-case basis?

For Atheists and Skeptics

- In your opinion, is it unethical for an unbelieving pastor to lie and say they believe when they don't? Are there any special circumstances or conditions that might change your answer?

- Would it be fair for an unbelieving pastor to view their role as that of a simple performer who's paid to provide crowds with a type of religious show that they've come to see? Would it make a difference whether the church was fundamentalist or liberal in orientation?

- Is there any way for a closeted unbelieving pastor to continue to preach without being completely dishonest? What if the pastor spoke only In metaphorical terms and no longer referenced the supernatural in literal terms during sermons? Would that make a difference?

Chapter Ten

.∎∎∎∎.∎.∎.∎'∎∎'∎∎

Shrapnel:
Picking Up the Pieces as They Continue to Explode

That fall I would finally admit to myself that I had indeed become an atheist. There wasn't any big event connected to it. I was just sitting at home in the living room when it hit me. After all those months, sitting right there is where it hit me that I had been playing games with myself, trying to force something that just wasn't. I realized it was now time to stand up once and for all, to quit running from the inevitable, to man up, stand up, and embrace the truth for what it was and without apology.

And there I rose from my seat, took to my feet, and declared fact over fiction to the audience surrounding me. I mean, the room was totally empty except for me and Charlie the dog. But that wasn't the point. The point was that I said it out loud. And I listened to myself say it loud and clear.

"I am an ATHEIST!"

And for the first time in over two years, I felt real. I felt real and honest and sane. I entered the next season before me, liberated from a mandated cognitive dissonance. For the first time, I was free to simply live and experience the world as I truly lived and experienced it. I was free to process my observations by no creed beyond that which made plain and simple sense. And more than anything else I was free to be me, to be and discover and explore who I truly was. Religion was gone. Doctrinal obligation and forced synthesis banished.

I was liberated.

And it felt beyond-words-rockstar-status amazing.

I was also flooded with feelings of joy. True overflowing and uncontrollable joy and excitement for the future. Sure, I had a lot of questions, but my mind was free to lead me wherever those questions and their answers should take me.

I said goodbye to God and have never looked back. Still now, I haven't prayed a single prayer since that day. It was over. The fight was finished. The wrestling complete. The torment extinguished. I had survived my hell. And I left its god right there in the pit. Sunshine on my face, I was moving forward on a new journey. I was about to reclaim my life.

That's what it felt like to finally embrace atheism.

The journey to reclaim my life, however, wasn't such an easy and exciting experience. It was like the part in a film where the climax has happened, when the big thing that the whole movie was driving toward explodes to fulfillment, but then you realize there's another whole forty-five minutes of movie left with another winding and tortuous plotline that you hadn't seen coming.

Well, once I had finally let go and quit clinging to the dead corpse of the ideas I'd called God, once I had gained the courage to finally walk away from it all, I began realizing that the fullness of the deconversion process would stretch out much further than simply embracing atheism. It would include the realignment of my entire life. And then I realized this process would finish neither quickly nor easily.

Every area of my life just seemed to unravel more and more.

But eventually things began to come back together again, in an even better and more honest and more sane way than ever before.

Let me explain.

You see, the full loss of my faith wasn't just the loss of faith itself. It was the loss of reality as I had ever known it. I may have finally admitted to myself that I had become an atheist, but the full process of my life's deconversion from Christianity was by no means complete. I had defined myself in Jesus since at least the age of twelve—for some twenty years. And my understanding of Christ had completely engulfed my own sense of self-identity.

And so I suddenly found myself churning in an ocean of question marks, awash in uncertainties about everything from the nature of my own personhood to the full arsenal of decisions that would need to be made as I marched into my future.

I've heard it said that something about the male brain makes men especially prone to defining themselves by their vocation or career. I'm not sure if this is true or not. Maybe it's due to engrained cultural boxes more than anything else. I know I've seen a good share of women that seem likewise defined by theirs. But it's also true that I've seen more than a couple males venture fresh into retirement only to find themselves on the brink of collapse as they struggle to rediscover life apart from the job they'd once devoted decades toward. For whatever reason, it seems a plumber might see plumbing as the definition of his existence, and when he can no longer plumb, he feels as if he's lost himself and is no longer sure of who or what he is. The same could be said of a painter or lawyer, a business owner or surgeon.

And this could certainly be said of me.

I was a pastor who could no longer pastor. But it was worse than that. Yes, I had lost my profession as a minister; this is true. But on the most fundamentally foundational level, I had seen myself as a Follower of Jesus Christ, born of the Spirit of God into a spiritually adoptive relationship with my God and Heavenly Father. I saw myself as a bondservant of the most high. I woke up every morning, took a knee in prayer, and asked God what he'd like me to sacrifice to him that day. I very intentionally lived each and every day in service to my Lord and regularly structured my life in a way that tried to cut away anything that might hold me back from a flawlessly spiritual lifestyle.

There's an evangelical tagline that says "I'm Third." It's supposed to be a rallying cry toward living out a priority of sacrifice. And it conveys an idea that my Number One priority ought always be to serve God first, followed by my Number Two priority, which is to serve everyone else in the world around me. It calls us to always and continually put their needs, desires, and preferences above my own. Only then, only if everyone else is completely indifferent to the choice at hand, *only then* do I live according to my own desires or preferences.

I'm Third.

And I really lived this way. Or at least tried to.

Every single day until I was thirty-three years old.

I learned to suppress all my desires, all my preferences, all my personal tastes. Now, I don't want to make this sound like more than it was. I did have opinions, likes, and preferences. A lot of them actually. And I voiced and advocated for them regularly. But if there was ever any conflict, I willingly submitted. At the very least, this was the ideal that I actively strived toward. And I wholeheartedly infused within my agenda for each day the desire to put the good of humanity before my own, the good of my nation before my own, the good of my community before my own, the good of my church before my own, the good of my family before my own. And if humanity or nation or community or church or family or GOD would be best served by my slaving away unto an early death, I saw this as my happy privilege.

In and through it all, I was defined by Jesus. I regularly reminded myself that I was nothing without him. And I honestly *truly* believed that this was true. I was nothing without Jesus.

And then I realized Jesus was fiction.

And soon after that I realized the call I had defined my life around was fiction.

This could mean only one thing.

That the boy who had always been nothing without Jesus was now simply nothing himself.

Early in my journey toward atheism, I had begun feeling duped by God. I know this doesn't make sense. *How could I feel duped by something that I didn't think existed?* But I did. I felt like I had been deceived, tricked, manipulated, brainwashed, bamboozled, swindled, hoodwinked, and basically just completely duped by God. Or by the idea of God. Or by religion.

So I no longer had any idea who I was or what I was. I wasn't sure what was supposed to fill the void left by the removal of faith, but something clearly felt missing. I guess most people just grow up seeing themselves primarily as a human and they just allow themselves the ability to self-define along the way. But my faith had defined me, and now that it was gone, I wasn't sure how to simply allow my simple selfness to bring redefinition. I would figure it out eventually, but it would take time, and it would be a rather painful journey.

I felt like my life had been hijacked.

And I frequently began wondering what I had missed out on. I would find myself dreaming of what might have been. *If I had never taken the Jesus train and never become a pastor, what might I have gone to college for? What might have become my profession?* When I was younger I had considered various careers: art, advertising, graphic design, even being a lawyer. *What might I be doing right now had it not been for the Jesus Hoax?*

And how much money would I be making? Would I still be living in an apartment, never having owned my own home and stuck with tens of thousands of dollars in consumer debt? Would I have a degree that was actually worth something—something I could put to use in getting a real job? Would I have options available to me beyond working in a restaurant the rest of my life? Would I be thirty-three years old and still clamoring to return to school for yet another set of degrees?

My career path had shifted quickly during the later months of 2012. Over the course of the summer, even as I was still transitioning out of my position at West Hills, I began questioning my ability to both return to school and also hold my finances together. Meanwhile, other opportunities were coming into focus at the steakhouse. They offered me an assistant general manager position at another location, which I immediately turned down since I was planning to return to school. But then as the weeks wore on, I started seeing large and gaping holes in my educational plan. *How did I really think I was to give a ThM and PhD the focus they needed while also working enough to feed my family and meet the increasing monetary demands of growing children with ambitious social and extracurricular lives?*

And so just two weeks after my final sermon, I abandoned my new career path. I dropped my classes at Trinity and announced my availability to begin management training at the steakhouse. I had already turned down the position just recently offered, but once another spot opened up, I wanted to be ready to move in. That was the new plan. And as it would turn out, the following year I would indeed accept a role as customer service manager in the steakhouse's Chicago location, the same position I had three times turned down way back in 2008.

But what did I want to do with the rest of my life?

Restaurant work is great for many people. The culinary and hospitality worlds are filled with some of the most innovative individuals on Earth, living out their passion and fulfilling their dreams. But this just wasn't for me. I was never excited by food and beverage. I mean, I loved *consuming* food and beverage, but I always struggled to care enough to commit details to memory. I hate cooking. I can do anything for a dollar if needed, but devoting the rest of my life's evenings, weekends, and holidays to the restaurant world sounded absolutely agonizing.

But taking a couple years to more or less punch a clock while I figured out what the hell to do with the rest of my life, that I could handle. Especially when it came to doing a job that I was honestly pretty good at.

And truth be told, I had absolutely no idea what I wanted to do next anyway.

Teaching had sounded so great while I was still in the pastorate. But now I had grown indifferent. I had some other ideas floating in my head, some community nonprofit work I might want to start up once I had the money to invest in it, some potential entrepreneurial ventures that sounded kind of exciting. And I had always been drawn to the world of politics. Or maybe some sort of artistic endeavor.

One evening I met with a friend for coffee at the Starbucks on North and Wells, and she saw one of those *For Dummies* books in my bag. It was called something obnoxious like *How to Become an Actor 101*. I told her that I was merely "curious" and that I was enrolled in a one-day acting workshop at Second City just to check it out. "Who knows?" I said.

Her eyes widened in disbelief.

"Seriously?" she demanded.

"Well, yeah . . ." I said as I seriously started to wish I had been carrying my old copy of Mortimer Adler's *How to Read a Book* instead.

"You're thirty-three years old," she reminded me, "and you seriously don't have *any* idea what you want to do with your life, do you?"

Some great observation skills, right there.

It's not like I really *wanted* to be an actor. I was just trying to be practical and thinking in terms of raw skill. Dramatic storytelling and creative expression were things I had done multiple times a week for over a dozen years. My skill set was certainly closer to acting than to building a damn computer. I didn't *want* to act. I just wanted to find something that paid bills without having to pay for another college degree.

But once again it was clear. I had grown pretty indifferent and apathetic and just didn't know what the hell I wanted to do with anything, much less with the rest of my entire life. And it wasn't just in terms of career. It was in terms of *everything*.

It was as if my capacity for excitement had died with my faith. All I wanted was the ability to survive each passing day, maybe find some time to read a good book and enjoy a nice glass of wine. But even those simple indulgences didn't seem to get me very far. All I could think of was this huge aching and throbbing tear through the center of my life that now felt beyond recovery. I had spent my whole life telling people that we were born with a God-shaped hole in our hearts that only he could fill. And now it really felt like this was the case.

As September spread into November, I began to wonder more about what life would have been like had I never come to faith. Sure, I was raised in a Christian culture and would have likely always embraced a mild belief in the Christian god's existence, but if I hadn't become extra-zealously evangelical the way I had and if my faith hadn't moved from the back burner to the front, how would it have been different?

Surrounded at the steakhouse by lots of twentysomethings, it seemed I was continually reminded of all the fun and games I had missed out on. I wondered how vastly different my college experience would have been had I attended a secular university instead of the Moody Bible Institute. I wondered about the parties and the women and the freedom to explore life and be young and take time to discover oneself.

How does the song go? "Living young and wild and free . . ."

And I began to wonder about dating and marriage. And I wondered, as much as I had always felt completely perfectly matched with Justina, whether our feelings of relational perfection were the simple byproduct of the belief that God Himself had appointed us to be together. That, and the fact that I had never actually dated anyone else. Ever.

And I began to wonder if, had it not been for my faith, would Justina and I have ever even gotten married. And the truth was, faith really did play a huge role in her even being willing to consider that first date. The truth is that had it not been for my extreme faith, she wouldn't have even looked at me. And so I found myself increasingly caught up in the fantasy of what it would have been like to have lived as a quote-unquote normal American twentysomething.

This all sounds horrible, I know.

Believe me, *I know.*

And it was horrible. And I take full responsibility for my actions—and the selfishness that ensued. I was less than loving or even fair to everyone in my life. And today I have no desire to shirk any responsibility for that. I'm not sitting here trying to put this on my recovery from religion. I was a grown adult in full control of my actions.

But it had occurred to me in the fall of 2012 that I had lived my entire life in a daily attempt to deny self. I *was* Third. I felt as if I had lived my whole life always looking for ways to put the desires and wishes of others ahead of my own.

And then it hit me.

I looked around and asked:

What the hell has all this sacrifice gotten me?

I've given up so much on an everyday basis, and what have I received in return?

What did those 12-, 15-, and 20-hour workdays at the church office achieve?

What did all my prayers accomplish?

And when I was so busy fussing over the joy of others who the hell was fussing over mine?

And so I concluded that I was going to start being selfish "for once in my life."

I felt duped by the idea of God and bitter that I had fallen for it. And I would reclaim my life by doing whatever the hell I wanted whenever the hell I wanted. I had always strived to eliminate selfishness but this would be my time of embrace.

Needless to say, a lot changed once I came to this point.

That fall, a friend shared some advice that her grandmother had given her back in high school. She had said that everyone goes wild at some point in their life. For those who work to suppress it when they are young, it ends up almost inevitably expressing itself when they are older, possibly in the form of a midlife crisis or something like that. But for those who enjoy the full freedom of youth and indulge in all its richness, that earlier experience makes it much more likely that they will enter adulthood knowing exactly what they want and how to get it. And they will live more stable and successful lives in the long run. *So go and do it now*, she sagely advised her granddaughter. *Live wild and free! Get it out of your system!* And then when you're an adult, settle down and live a successful and confident life.

Oh, to be told that in high school! Oh, to be given such permission to live life and experiment and explore the depths of wherever it takes you!

Now, I'm not exactly sure how well that grandmother's advice corresponds with the most trusted sociological or psychological findings. But at the time, it really made sense to me. It was exactly what I was feeling. I had been given different advice, and now I was feeling trapped and cornered. I felt like the world was suddenly so much bigger than I had ever imagined possible. It was an exciting world, and I was missing out. Though I had squandered so much of my youth, I still had a window of opportunity. But this too was closing fast. Give it another decade or so and my options would look a lot different.

This was my one life to live.

And it would all be over in the blink of an eye or in the time it takes to utter any other such cliché.

That winter, I told Justina I wanted to separate. It's true that I had increasingly felt like she and I had two completely different visions for our postpastoral years—*we had both noticed this*. But even more than that, I just didn't want to be married anymore.

People who have never met her often assume that she was the one who left me. They often assume this because of what has become the stereotyped situation where the still-Christian spouse just can't handle being married to an atheist and files for divorce, citing such reasons as *spiritual abandonment* or a breaking of vows made "before God." But ours was not such a case. It wasn't her. It was all me. I was the asshole.

Let me repeat that again: *I was the asshole.*

She wanted to seek out marital counseling, and I agreed, pending two requirements. One, that the therapist not be a Christian—or at least not one with a traditional Christian view of marriage. And, two, that the counseling not include any overriding agenda that sees marriage as an eternal covenant to be salvaged at all costs. An acceptable angle would be one that seeks to find common ground and bring us both to a place of psychological and emotional health, and that only then would determine whether we were still compatible as a couple. That kind of agenda would be fine.

And eventually we discovered the work of Doctor Ray and Reverend Jean, a wonderful couple who were both therapists and ran a practice together specializing in this very thing. The therapy featured a two-part approach where either all four of us met together to work through relationship stuff or Justina and I attended individual therapy sessions with Jean and Ray, respectively. They did include a hearty helping of spirituality of Eastern origin—a mix of Daoism, Buddhism, and Zoroastrianism, which rounded out their Gestalt and Jungian clinical philosophies. But one thing was clear, the therapy definitely wasn't Christian and it didn't import any of that marriage-is-an-eternal-mandate stuff.

And this wonderful couple was really quite amazing. Seriously, the powerful experience they provided played an incredibly constructive role in both of our lives as Justina and I dealt with years of baggage and worked our way toward individual health. And along that way, I even thought maybe we'd end up staying together in the end.

But new complications were brewing. As helpful as the whole process was, and as instrumental as it would prove long-term, I started facing some compulsions that were not finding an immediate fix in therapy. And I wasn't quite sure what to do about them.

It's to these ongoing complications we now turn.

Questions for the Dialogue

Topics of discussion may vary widely here. But let's get some ideas on the table.

For Everyone

- What do you think of the feeling of freedom described here that can follow one's embrace of atheism? What implications might this have on the role of faith?

- What do you make of the mess that can follow one's departure from faith? How might this support the case for faith? How might it refute it?

- What could have been handled better in this part of the story? What was most troubling?

- If a friend came to you who was in a similar situation, what advice would you give them? How would you hope to impact their ultimate decisions?

Chapter Eleven

Claustrophobia:
The Crushing Weight of Questions Unanswered

It started off mild and quickly grew obsessive. I faced the growing compulsion to run and get away. I felt trapped, but it was more than this. To this day I struggle for the best words to describe what I was experiencing over those months. But it was almost like a panicked trance. The kind in which you might suddenly find yourself driving a car, heading nowhere without reason. Just driving without a destination. Just driving to get away. Feeling claustrophobic and like your life depended on you just getting the hell outa there.

But it didn't start off that way.

I suppose it simply started with a lot of questions about who I was without my faith. The same kind of questions that had started bothering me in previous months, the ones we're probably getting sick of reading about. And believe me, I was getting sick of them as well.

Who am I?

What am I?

What do I believe in?

Do I believe in anything?

How do I get my life back on track?

And what does back on track even look like?

And since I had always been such an intentional and driven person—and since that sense of intentionality and drive were so fundamentally attached to my theology—I was overcome with the immediate need to completely reconstruct a new set of views. *How could I still be intentional and driven if I had absolutely no idea what to be intentional and driven about?*

And so along with my faith and my identity, I also lost all sense of purpose and meaning and motivation and intentionality and drive.

My Christian theology had given me such confident and immovable answers to life's biggest questions. The Bible held the indisputable keys to unlocking the answers of right and wrong, of ethics and morality, and of the purpose and meaning of humanity. And I had had those answers. But now they were gone. And I had to start all over in an effort to construct new answers, and now everything was on the table. I didn't even know if there were answers to those questions anymore. But I felt the need to at least know whether or not I thought there were any to be known.

I felt the need to reconstruct my entire worldview from scratch.

And now. *Right now.*

Meanwhile, life kept pushing forward.

Family needs. Marriage needs. Job and financial needs.

As someone who used to not even get out of bed before asking God's permission and who now found himself with his entire framework ripped apart, I was beginning to feel like I couldn't even function. Life kept moving faster and faster, but I didn't know how to keep up. I needed a pause button. Something that would give me a moment to step aside and catch my breath.

I had always scoffed at the idea of a midlife crisis. It was the domain of the weak. It was for those who floated through life without a sense of purpose. For those who lacked all sense of initiative or personal responsibility. It was for those who had never learned how to get their act together.

And now I was the one who was floating.

Or, more accurately, the one being swept away by the torrent.

I needed to get away.

I needed to run. *I couldn't stay.* I needed to run and get away.

Now. *Right now.*

My mind wouldn't let me rest until I had done so.

And so I began dreaming of what it might be like to actually literally run away, to just flee everything I knew of life and to start over from scratch. Just skip town and never look back. New name, new identity, new life. New job, new home, new circle of friends. A witness protection program sounded simply magical. And Chris McCandless had become my hero.

But at the same time, I knew it wasn't *really* what I actually wanted.

I possessed enough objective introspection to diagnose it as a phase of some kind. And that once I could have all my questions and curiosities satisfied I would likely start feeling quite normal again. The running itself would serve as nothing more than a mere bandage to greater needs.

And more importantly, what really ultimately held me back was knowing the implications such a disappearance would have on Justina and the children. Those precious and amazing daughters of ours were my life and joy in so many ways. The little bit of happiness I still felt able to enjoy seemed to come from them. And I knew that if I ever did vaporize into the hilltops without a word of warning it would have the potential to destroy them emotionally for the rest of their lives. I couldn't do that to them. And I really didn't want to be separated from them like that—*especially not forever.* So I wasn't sure how to process the barrage of things I was feeling, but I knew that running away and disappearing was definitely not the solution.

And then I started waking up suddenly in the middle of the night with a panicked compulsion to jump in my car and disappear. Right then and there.

Just go! Now!

It didn't happen often. Only three or four times spread out over a month or so.

And then one day it happened for real. I was overcome by a few moments of hypnotic disregard, and I pulled onto Interstate 90 and started driving toward Wisconsin. I felt like I was in a trance, and in my half-crazed state I honestly wasn't sure I would ever return to Illinois again. I really didn't even care.

But in less than an hour, a debate had arisen within me. And thankfully the side of me that favored a life of sanity and seeing my children again won the battle that day. But those moments scared the bejesus out of me. I felt as if my mind had slipped out of its proper state.

And I feared what might happen the next time.

I figured the best way to get to the root of the problem and make sure I didn't actually up and disappear for real one day was to take some time away before it got that bad. Almost like a mini-disappearance, but a controlled one. Like an extended retreat from my real life. I had hoped that if I took a few months to move out of the house and get my own place that this might provide the space I needed to really think through all the answers to my questions and rediscover myself. And since Justina and I had already been discussing divorce, this would provide a trial along those lines as well.

So the two of us sat down at a local pancake house one Saturday morning to discuss the arrangements. I would be leaving, but we had planned for it to merely be a temporary separation. We tried to make all the proper preparations and go about everything "the right way"—if there is such a thing. What possessions would go where and for how long. How much money would go this way and that. And then we picked a date. April 1, 2013.

April Fool's Day.

I attempted making bad jokes about April Fool's Day being the day she would get the fool out of the house. But she never laughed because they were never funny.

We planned the separation with a six-month timetable. And then we shortened it to four. We would touch base throughout the process and see one another regularly when passing the kids back and forth. And in July we would meet to decide whether or not we wanted to reunite and get back together. That was the plan.

I honestly hoped I'd be ready and able to return at the end of those months. Get it out of my system and then come back. I *wanted* to *want* to come back. And I thought that after a few months away from the love of my life, all those old feelings would revive and we'd be back in business—that I would also be able to return to civilian life having rebuilt my perspective, feeling once again alive and ready to charge forth into a bold new chapter.

At least that's how I envisioned it at the beginning.

I found a small studio apartment on a dumpy block in Chicago's Uptown neighborhood. And the word *dumpy* makes it sound better than it really was. Let's just say it wasn't the greatest of places to live. But the rent was dirt cheap, allowing me some time to figure out my finances while I transitioned. I was staying on the tenth floor of the Lawrence House, a building that was under, shall we say, special status. From what the manager had told me, it used to be overridden with drugs and gangs, but he was brought in with a reputation for clearing out the riffraff and getting things in order. There was 24-hour in-house security along with a Chicago Police Department squad car parked out front from 6-9 p.m. each evening, just to make sure everything remained calm and above board.

But still, the building seemed mostly populated with those who would otherwise be homeless. I was often told by other residents that I must be the only person there with a steady job. Many who lived in our building had clear mental health concerns. My children still talk about the time they saw a man use the restroom in the downstairs lobby—the kind of use that involves dropping one's pants to squat—only in this case the "restroom" was actually the middle of the lobby itself. And then there was the large and robust woman from Uganda who started stalking me and accusing me of trying to have invisible brain-sex with her animal-spirit. And on a whole other level, I'll never forget the howling screams of other residents that would echo through the night.

Needless to say, I looked for alternative housing as fast as possible. *Talk about the need to get away! Now—right now!*

But it wasn't always bad. Sure, the cockroaches weren't always the best of company, but for the few months that I stayed there, I really was able to make the most of it. I just kept to myself and spent most of my time outside.

My time in seclusion was basically divided into two very different lifestyles. Or maybe just two sides to one dysfunctionally balanced lifestyle. I'm not sure. Time outside of the steakhouse was devoted to rebuilding that sense of perspective and identity. I rarely watched television and hardly ever spoke. I loved the silence. I would go for long meandering walks all day every day until it was time to head in for my afternoon or evening work shift. Being only three or four blocks from Chicago's lakeshore, I would spend countless hours walking up and down the lakefront, sitting, thinking, observing, reflecting. I would watch other people living life, families barbequing near the beach and Saturday morning youth soccer games. I would just sit there on the sidelines of life and watch the world as an outsider working to assess the meaning of it all.

I was bombarded with phone calls, emails, and social media messages, those asking a million and a half questions about all that had happened and wanting to know what the hell was going on. I couldn't take it. I defriended 90 percent of my Facebook contacts. For months I refused to return the phone calls of even my closest family members. The only exception was Justina and our daughters. Spending time with my girls, then ages eight and ten, remained the one constant I refused to give up. They stayed with me every other weekend, and we would go on great adventures together, visiting museums, seeing shows, and eating at all our favorite restaurants. But beyond them, I cut everyone else out. I couldn't handle seeing anyone else. I couldn't bear the thought of their questions. And I didn't have the answers yet anyway.

I spent my days reading anything I could get my hands on. I wanted to encounter as much as I could from a wide range of sources. Everything from presidential biographies to classic literary works. My therapist Doctor Ray continued feeding me the likes of Dan Millman, don Miguel Ruiz, and Eckhart Tolle. I also picked up first readings of Friedrich Nietzsche and Christopher Hitchens. Eventually, I would make my way to this evolutionary biologist named Richard Dawkins and stumble upon someone named Dan Barker, another former preacher whom I had never heard of but one who, like me, had also found it impossible to keep believing in God. This was the first time I had ever read stuff by other atheists, and they were proposing answers to lots of the very questions that were plaguing me. It was marvelous and I relished each page of every book.

I also wrote hundreds of pages of my own over those months. I began journaling extensively and would find tremendous power in its ability to help me sort out all that was churning back and forth in my mind and heart. And that summer I would follow Doctor Ray's suggestion that I begin recording my deconversion story. Though it would take awhile to manifest themselves, serious steps were being taken to find a new anchor for the reality I now found myself living within. And it was as refreshing as the cool springtime breeze rolling off Lake Michigan.

But then there was that other side of this whole journey. I had an ongoing desire to taste all the experiences that I had missed out on over the years, all the little indulgences that life had to offer. To reenact my would-be twenties and reinvent beyond them.

And so I partied to no end.

I went out nearly every night after work. If there's one perk to downtown steakhouse life, it's the VIP access you have to any bar or club around the city. Connections are everywhere. You treat them well, and they will take care of you. If you work a normal 9–5 M–F job, you might polish off the workday with your office mates and a Happy Hour beer. But if you work in the restaurant and hospitality industry, you're not getting off until midnight, and Happy Hour doesn't end until two or four or even five in the morning. And that summer, this is what I was doing three to five nights a week. And even still, I can count on one hand how many times I waited in a line at a club or had to pay a cover charge.

That's how easily accessible it all is. That's how effortless the indulgence. And any experience, any indulgence you might be looking for, it's all there. With the reach of a hand, at the touch of a finger. And suddenly, everything I had ever dreamed of or fantasized about was right there. Drinking until my heart's content. Indulgence to the fullest. And being completely honest, it felt marvelous.

I couldn't even keep up with the blur. Drink after drink. Club after club. Night after night.

One evening in particular I was hanging out with friends at Paris Club. And the next moment, a blonde European bombshell was taking me by the hand and leading me out the door, down the alley, around the corner, and right up to some newly renovated club I hadn't yet heard of. It was called The Underground, and it was indeed underground. My new nameless bombshell friend led me through this sea of hundreds of people waiting to get in, led me right up to the gate and told the bouncer, "He's with me."

The next day as I spoke with a friend at the steakhouse, she marveled at the fact that I was able to get inside since it was apparently the club's opening weekend and had quickly been declared the hottest spot in Chicago.

Seriously, I had no idea how any of this was happening.

I was just along for the ride and loving the change of scenery.

And that was my summer. Nights would be spent drinking up every moment. I'd go home and sleep for a few hours, and then get up to walk around the city and think the deep things of life and work to recreate my perspective. It was slow coming. But I was beginning to learn to feel again. The numbness was beginning to thaw. And I was starting to get somewhere.

But by this time, the march toward divorce was already well under way. When Justina had asked me just six weeks into the separation if I was ready to come back, the sad reality is that I just wasn't. I'd later wish that I had been. And I would get there eventually. But only six weeks into the separation, I yet remained that numb asshole who was just bumping around in the dark and still a long way off from stability.

But Justina was awesome. And she was trying to be patient.

So she came back a few weeks after that. And I wasn't ready then either.

Or in the few weeks after that.

And eventually, well, eventually, she had to make a choice.

She was trying to wait for the four months to pass. I'm sure she really honestly was. But you have to consider all she had been through since I first led her to the Jesus train in high school and how the complex dynamics of our relationship had affected her. Over time she had grown to recognize her own identity had been completely wrapped up within mine. This here is the devastation of an evangelical social structure at its finest. And so just as I was struggling to redefine myself apart from faith in God, she was in the throes of figuring out how to redefine herself apart from her husband.

And, from what I understand, she had come to a point where she needed to prove to herself that she would be just fine without me, that her own identity was more than just being my wife. It had kinda felt as if she wouldn't be able to survive without me there by her side, but she was tenacious and determined to prove to herself that she could. That I did not define her and that she would indeed survive with or without me.

And so rather than waiting for me to come back and break it off in July, and rather than waiting around with her entire life on hold while I "discovered myself" and tramped all over the city, she decided to rise up and take action herself.

And that summer she filed for divorce. And she filed a special exemption allowing her to bypass Cook County's normal two-year predivorce separation period.

The divorce was finalized on August 29, 2013.

As that summer faded into autumn, I was finally beginning to gain a sense of normalcy again. I had found a new apartment just a block off Lake Michigan with an amazing eleventh-story view of Lincoln Park and Montrose Beach. It was still pretty small and a far cry from my ultimate goal, but it was a step and one that I was pretty pleased with.

And that September, the management position I was preparing for at the steakhouse opened up and I slid right in. I wasn't sure where all this was going to lead, but it sure felt good to see some things beginning to move positively in my life.

Things were really starting to look up. I still felt totally isolated in my disbelief, but I was beginning to reestablish old relationships and return some of those phone calls. A new worldview was coming together, and I was starting to feel at home in my own skin. I was going out less, working out more, and actually sleeping once in awhile. Life was moving along pretty well for the most part. I still had my days. But I was learning to smile a little more often, and the smile was genuine.

And then the absolute greatest thing happened.

It was an unexpected encounter that finally showed me I was most certainly not alone.

And it's this event that propels our story to its *rise above* . . .

Questions for the Dialogue

So here's the part where we dialogue about all the decisions that could have been made differently and all the ways this transition could have gone smoother.

For Everyone

- What do you think of this transition? It was certainly messy, but do you think it was necessarily messy given the circumstances or do you think poor decisions made it a lot worse than it needed to be? How so?

- How would you encourage or advise a friend going through a similar situation?

For Believing Christians

- To what degree do you believe the issues here are spiritual in nature? To what degree are they psychological? Can they be both? What would be the best course of action for a nonbeliever experiencing such a crisis?

For Atheists and Skeptics

- To what degree do you think the issues here are psychological in nature? Can you see why some Christians might want to explain the problem in terms of spirituality? What would you say in response?

PART FOUR:
THE RISE ABOVE

Chapter Twelve

Finding Home:
Discovering Hope in Community

My entire life had been shaped by my faith. But as of December 2013, it had most forcefully fallen. And there I had sat, right there in its tattered remains. But then, something amazing happened. Like the rising sun in all its shining glory, my life encountered a new uplift. It's here where my story connected with the stories of countless others. It's here where I began to realize with the utmost of clarity that my story was more than just my own.

I had seen on Facebook a couple weeks earlier that an old friend from Bible college was going to be in town. He and I had lived on the same floor during undergrad, and though I had never known him really well, he had always seemed like a cool enough guy who was easy to get along with. He had held this nontraditional don't-take-me-too-seriously vibe, perfectly complemented by a huge mass of long and tightly kinked hair and a scraggly beard. He had left Moody early way back then and was now working toward a PhD in linguistics. So basically he was one of those brilliant geniuses who just wanted to hang out and be an eternal student telling great jokes and laughing at everyone else's. And through the years we had become Facebook friends and somehow kept in touch.

His name was Scott.

And one day Scott posted something about coming to Chicago.

And I thought to myself, *Damn, it might be kinda cool to meet up with this guy*

Scott. I haven't seen anyone from my Moody days in forever, and I don't see him as the kinda guy to bring any judgments against me for being an atheist . . . And honestly, he had never struck me as all that religious himself.

So I reached out to him, and we set something up. We met at the ever-popular Stout Barrel House and Galley, located right around the corner from the steakhouse. It was late in the evening on a weeknight when I ran over and caught up with him after finishing my double shift. It was a quiet night, and we sat at the bar with the entire place to ourselves.

For two hours we consumed brew after tasty brew while catching up on all things since Moody. We laughed and joked and made fun of the kinds of things that a carefree life obligates one to laugh at and joke about. And of course he asked about my deconversion, and I told him a good share of the details. He received them effortlessly, and we mused on the unpredictability of life.

And then out of nowhere and as if it was nothing, Scott mentioned a private Facebook group that he was a member of. It was a group of current and former Moody students who had moved beyond theological belief as sanctioned by our alma mater. It was true that most had stuck with Christianity, simply trading in the conservative Moody version for something a bit more progressive. But others had evolved into Buddhism or other less organized spiritualties. One had gone the Muslim route. And for a few of them, wouldn't you know it, they had left religion altogether. Atheists and agnostics. And some of them, like this scholarly author guy named Bart Ehrman, were even public about it.

Anyway, this group of two-hundred-plus Moodies had come together to create a beautiful safe-haven oasis of nonjudgmentalness. Many of them had grown up in fundamentalist Christian homes and regularly faced a reality of ostracism, condemnation, and isolation for their adjustments to faith. Most of them weren't even atheists. They still believed in some version of God, just not the right one. And for this they were vilified.

They called themselves the Moody Bible Institute Heretics. And they wore the title proudly. Moody may condemn them. But sometimes you find things more important than the approval of others. And the community found in this group was just such a thing.

From what I was told, Moody had apparently tried to shut the group down. But without success. This is still America after all, and the religious clutches over society aren't quite as severe as some would imagine them to be. But there were rumors of spies being sent into the group to collect information. And, I learned, some current students had even succumbed to the pressure and resigned membership.

So that night at Stout, Scott was telling me about this group. And about how cool it was. And about how people would post about really personal and intimate life conflicts that they couldn't share with anyone else. And how the group would rally around them for support and encouragement and community. He said it was really cool and thought I might benefit from it.

And then he pulled out his phone and added me.

And at that very moment, I became a Moody Heretic.

And it really was a pretty cool little group. The kind of conversations that disturbed me the most were the ones where women would discuss the kind of sexual repression that had become deep-seated as a result of their religious indoctrination. It was a kind of sexual repression that went far beyond anything I had personally seen before, but it seemed to be remarkably common within our group. It produced the kind of sexual dysfunction that left far too many of these dear women so ashamed and disgusted by their own sexuality that they couldn't even have sex with their husbands without feeling physically ill. I couldn't believe the horror. So twisted had their theology become that the capacity for these beautiful and amazing women to enjoy the human pleasures of sex had been apparently destroyed. Even after they had left their oppressive theology behind, the psychological ramifications continued to haunt them. That's how deeply the abuse had embedded itself.

And this was just one of the results of such religious fundamentalism.

It is true that this group had learned to truly be there for one another, even if separated by thousands of miles. Connected through digitized smart screens, they had learned to support one another and care for one another and share in each other's burdens. They had learned to build true community. And it came so easily. So naturally and so effortlessly. Because of all that was shared through the Moody experience and because of all the evangelical-fundamentalist baggage that it represented.

And it was here that I too relearned community. It was here where I began to truly understand that I was not alone. There were others just like me. Now it's true that most of them weren't atheists. And only a few of them had ever been pastors. But at least we shared a thread of common experience, walking together while collectively recovering from religion.

And that's how it started.

But we were only getting started.

Because it would be just a few months later, just as I was really getting into the whole Moody Heretics thing and finding connections with so many wonderful new friends, that I received a private message from a fellow Moody Heretic. And this message would serve as another link in the chain helping me find even greater post-Christian community.

The message came in June 2014. And my new Heretic friend introduced herself as an active Presbyterian pastor whose faith had fallen apart in similar fashion to my own. She had seen some of my Facebook postings and wanted to reach out to say hello. But she was also reaching out for another reason, one beyond the mere saying of hello. She wanted to tell me about another group that she had also recently joined, one that she thought I might benefit from as well.

It was called The Clergy Project. She sent me a link, and I said I'd check it out. It took me a couple weeks to get around to it, but eventually I made my way over to ClergyProject.org. And the more I read, the more perfect this group seemed. I didn't quite realize it at the time, but it was exactly what I was looking for.

In March 2011, The Clergy Project had been launched in an effort to provide a safe, anonymous online community for current and former religious professionals who no longer held supernatural beliefs. Within the safe space of a private online forum, project participants found a network of support and community as they freely discussed and assisted one another in the challenges related to the leaving of ministry and the establishment of life beyond faith. Just as the name implies, The Clergy Project had begun as a mere *project*, one forged by the collaborative efforts of Dan Barker, Richard Dawkins, Daniel Dennett, Linda LaScola, and others—a project featuring fifty-two charter members. But by the summer of 2014, The Clergy Project had grown to become its own self-sustaining nonprofit organization with well over six hundred registered participants spread across the globe in more than thirty countries.

It was just like the Moody Heretics but larger. And rather than only a few atheists and a small dash of former pastors among its membership, this time they were *all* nonbelieveres and *100 percent* of them had been clergy of some variation or another. A full third were still in their religious professions and deeply closeted in their disbelief. And like me they had often felt completely isolated in their atheism, with this project serving as their sole source of support. It was exactly what I needed, and I jumped right into the application and screening process.

And then just like that, I was suddenly surrounded by an incredible network of support that attended to every facet of life, providing peer-to-peer guidance on everything from employment assistance to issues dealing with religious friends and family to questions about when and how to come out as an atheist publicly.

It was here with The Clergy Project where I found a sense of community that I hadn't yet seen. It was here where it truly and fully sank in that I was no longer alone. And that I actually never was.

But even more than this, I gained a very real sense of *hope*. I know not all post-Christians like to use this word, but for me personally, I find it as powerful as ever. If hope is the anticipation of a better day, that's exactly what I so desperately needed. It's true that things had already started to reassemble themselves in my life and mind, but I still had a long way to go. And sometimes it was hard to believe things could ever actually be great again. I had still been skeptical that life would ever truly be worth living again.

But it was here in these discussions with my new friends and in reading their stories where I was able to see over and over how nonbelieving pastors, rabbis, monks, and imams—*people just like me*—were actually rebuilding their lives. And they were doing it successfully.

I was also beginning to come across all kinds of books by former clergypersons who had left the faith and gone on to rebuild their lives. First I read Dan Barker's *Godless*, the 2008 account of his personal deconversion story. And then John Compere's *Towards the Light* and Jerry DeWitt's *Hope After Faith*. From there, I kept finding more and more books to stabilize and rebalance my perception of life postfaith.

But mostly, this sense of hope came through the simple realization that I was not alone. There were others. Hundreds of them. Well, hundreds who had found their way to The Clergy Project. But also an untold mass of thousands—perhaps *hundreds* of thousands—of others still out there and just as obliviously alone as I had been just a few months prior.

In this simple realization, I felt empowered. The task of rebuilding my life was normalized to just another set of tasks that everyday people just like me have to tackle and complete every single day. It wasn't something to cry about and become immobilized by. It was something to push through and grow stronger from. Just as all these other postfaith pastors were doing. The circumstances I had found myself in, though not ideal, were not hastening the end of my life. No, far from it. I began to realize that this was simply the beginning of a whole new chapter. And that if I could but simply harness the energy, it could be a pretty damn good chapter at that.

So no more pity parties.

No more dwelling on all I had left behind.

No more entertaining slideshows of All That Could Have Been.

No, no, no . . . In the summer of 2014 I had found a new invigoration to stand up and capture my life anew. To not only *seize the day*, but to seize *my entire life*. And once I came to this place and arrived at this mindset, everything else started falling right in line.

And all as a result of *community*.

Questions for the Dialogue

This story shows us an example of the role community—even online community—can play in our individual lives. Let's talk about that.

For Everyone

- What groups (civic, religious, etc.) do you participate in, be it online or on location? How does your involvement benefit you? Or, in other words, why are you there? Would you say you "identify" with these groups? And how so? Does this participation make you stronger, healthier, happier, or simply more sane?

- What do you think about the two online groups featured in this story? What are the implications of their presence?

For Believing Christians

- Of all the various people you interact with in a typical week, what percentage of them seem to be vocal Christians? What percentage of them are vocal Muslims? What percentage vocal Buddhists? Hindus? Zoroastrians? Yoruba? And what percentage of them are vocal atheists? What effect do you think those percentages have on your lifestyle?

- To what extent do you think your belief system is shaped by the cultural context you live within? If you arrived at conclusions that ran contrary to everyone around you, how easily do you think you could be open and vocal about your convictions? Would you feel the need to find a small group of others who identified with your same convictions?

For Atheists and Skeptics

- Do you know of other disbelievers in your own local community? Are they good friends or family members? How might this make a difference in the role of skepticism in your own life?

- What is your reaction to the presence of the online groups in the story? Have you gotten involved with any online groups for nonbelievers? What role do you think these groups might play in your own identification as an atheist or skeptic?

Chapter Thirteen

Today and Forward:
My Life and the Humble Humanist Ideal

You might remember Rob from my Bethel Church days, the pastor who was one of my closest friends and with whom I had kept in regular touch throughout the downward spiral of my faith. He was the only person who had been completely in the loop the entire time. You might also remember that we would meet for lunch every couple months and that he was always a rock-solid source of support throughout that time. Well, after I left the church and came out as an atheist, he and I lost track of one another for about a year and a half. I had blamed it on being busy, but really I just pushed him off for the same reason I had pushed everyone else off.

But then in the later months of 2013, as I was trying to reestablish some of those old connections, Rob and I finally sat down for another cup of long-overdue coffee. We met one evening late into the night at that Second City Starbucks on North and Wells.

Now, I know I've already told you how amazing this guy was, but seriously he and his friendship ought to stand as evidence that there really are open-minded evangelical pastors out there who won't automatically condemn you and who will still truly love you even as you stop believing in Jesus. It might not be easy to find them, mind you, but they're out there nonetheless, scattered about the nation in tight corners and tiny crevices.

Our conversation looked much like any other conversation with a good friend you hadn't seen in much too long of a time. And he wanted to be that good-listening-ear kind of friend. I gave him all the updates, and then we moved on to talk about all the other kinds of subject matters we usually liked to talk about.

But at one point he said the perfect thing. The fact that he was still a believer and still a pastor created a potential elephant-in-the-room kind of vibe. And so he addressed it, of course, but in the most Rob-like of ways.

"Just in case you're wondering if I'm going to preach to you or try to say something to get you to think about stuff in a certain way, you need to know that I respect you way too much for that, man. I was there with you through the breakdown of your faith, and I saw you wrestle through it with as much honesty and integrity and emotional agony as I've ever seen in anyone. You know your Bible as much as I do and far more than most, so what could I possibly have to say to you about those things."

Then he meandered a bit with a pause. "Honestly, I don't really know what to make of everything that's happened. But I know that I trust you to navigate your life the best way possible. Am I praying for you? Of course I am. But I'm not going to be so arrogant as to try to get you to bow your head and pray with me or something here tonight. Just know that I'm here for you and that though we might disagree on things, I hope we can still be great friends who are real with one another and who truly love one another for who we truly are underneath the surface."

Nothing condescending or arrogant in the least. He had been one of my truest friends, and even now he was there for me. He laid low when I needed space and then returned without reservation, hesitation, or judgment as soon as I needed him.

And we hung out as the old friends that we were. And we also talked about his life and the thick of things that he was going through. It was real. And it was refreshing to have it once again.

But then he said something more. Hovering over hours-old and hours-cold coffee, Rob said something that spoke more powerfully than anything else. He said he was glad to see I was "still the same guy," essentially the same person I had always been. He outlined how I was still the same great father. Still the same well-meaning individual who was inherently loving and respecting and easy-going and mild-mannered. I still had the same sense of humor and still enjoyed the same kinds of films and music and books. I still loved to talk politics and culture and art. I still loved humanity and wanted to play a constructive role in the world around me.

He said he had never really bought into the religious mythology that says all atheists are inherently evil and selfish and wicked and that they are Communists and the Destroyers of All Civilization. He said he had never bought into that kind of categorical condemnation. But he also admitted that, leading up to our coffee reunion, he wasn't exactly sure how I had turned out. He feared that maybe, just maybe, my life had been flipped upside down so much that I had transformed into a cruel and heartless social villain, one who no longer wanted anything to do with his children or had devolved into an angry-yelling-and-screaming kind of social troll.

And he said he was glad to see that I hadn't. Despite everything I had faced, and despite the rugged journey I had found myself on, he was pleased to see that my true self had come out very much the same as what it had always been.

On the other side of all the apparent changes, very little was actually all that different.

I was the same Drew.

Rediscovering Humanism

Once stumbling into The Clergy Project in the summer of 2014, my participation grew rather steadily. I was also blogging regularly about my deconversion experience and all the various facets of life that my deconversion had affected. And along the way, it was suggested to me that I reach out to the American Humanist Association and maybe seek an endorsement from The Humanist Society, which would allow me to perform nonreligious weddings and funerals and whatnots. I wasn't entirely sure I wanted to start doing weddings again, but it was the concept of *humanism* that piqued my interest more than anything else.

I had always liked the concept of humanism. As a more progressive evangelical pastor, I had used the term humanist to describe both myself and the Christian perspective I advocated. As *evangelicals* we believed every word of the Bible as truth, but as *Christian humanists*, we believed that God was working for our good and betterment. And we believed that our role in society was to be advocates of social justice and equality. We believed God had appointed us to love and never condemn, to build up and never tear down, and to always work toward the bigger picture of a thriving humanity instead of short-term quick fixes. That was Christian humanism.

And I had nearly forgotten all about it.

Until I encountered the *secular humanism* of the American Humanist Association. In many ways it was just the same as my humanism of before. It was a striving for the big-picture betterment of a thriving humanity. But this time it was free of dogma and of the need to conform to any particular religious text or theology. Free to simply embrace *humanity*'s power of observation and reason. Free to elevate *all* humanity in *every* way without constraint by the pressures of doctrine or discipline.

And this new brand of humanism was exactly what I was eager to embrace all over again. Pro-observation. Pro-science. Pro-reason. Pro-personal worth and dignity. Pro-liberty and freedom. Pro-responsibility. Pro-community. Pro-empowerment. Pro-justice. Pro-environment.

Pro-*humanity*.

Truly, *the big-picture betterment of a thriving humanity*. Or at least that's how I began describing it. And in many ways, it embodied everything I had ever been passionate about. The same Drew, just without the Jesus.

The Joy of All Freethinking Joys

I used to say that Jesus was my utmost joy and source of all strength. But now today my utmost joy and source of all strength is indisputably those two beautiful and amazing little girls I call my daughters. Though, they're not so little anymore.

My teenage eldest is a powerhouse leader with a wonderfully irreverent sense of humor. In the first grade she began giving up her recess time to assist a special-education class. Two years after that, she became a student senator. Ridiculously smart and undeterred in accomplishing her goals, she told me one day in May about how she was combing back over every question she'd missed on all her tests for the entire year in order to commit the real answers to memory.

This is because she's already planning for college and promises she's going to make so much money, she'll be able to stick me away inside the best nursing home available. We laugh about her desire to *stick me away*, but she swears she's one to keep her promises.

Extending beyond the realm of college planning and money making, she's also a fierce athlete who played varsity volleyball as an eighth grader. *I didn't even know that was possible.* But seriously she's incredibly driven and stops at nothing to achieve her ever-advancing goals. Ever. And honestly, I'm daily amazed by her.

My youngest, herself about to become a teenager, has always been the performer and entertainer in the family. Dance class and gymnastics seem to excite her like nothing else. But she also just loves people and has a breathtaking sense of empathy. Also having served in the student senate, her young heart is probably bigger than all the rest of ours combined. And she will stop at nothing to come alongside others and help them know how valued and uniquely amazing they are.

She also came to me last year, saying she was hungry for a new challenge, and asked me to show her how to publish an e-book. With minimal help from me, she wrote it, formatted it, and posted it on Amazon. And then a print edition was requested by a therapist on the East Coast. And so we made one of those as well.

Basically, I view it as my parental responsibility to not only equip and empower my kids to become the greatest version of themselves—*however they may desire to individually define that greatness*—but to also celebrate them and cheer them on as loudly as possible.

Can you hear me cheering yet?

Am I loud enough?

But from before they were born, Justina and I have always been committed to raising our girls as freethinkers, teaching them *how* to think, not *what* to think. And in our family's latest season, this commitment has only expanded. True, the divorce has made certain things a bit messy, but the interaction we share has remained pretty good—certainly more than mere civility. And we continue to work together constructively as co-parents, providing our daughters with two different freethinking homes to draw from as they independently craft their own conclusions with our full support.

And I think it needs to be said. If either of our girls were to grow up and decide to embrace Christianity, I'd be fine with that. I'd just want it to be a conscious decision based on what they've seen at work both out in the world and within their inner selves. As long as they're living lives of joy and self-acceptance, I will be a happy man. And I'm confident Justina will be pretty pleased as well.

Transitioning to Today

In many ways blogging led to a more connected life. Once I started sharing parts of my story back in 2014, others in situations like mine started reaching out. They asked for my thoughts on this and that. They'd share parts of their stories with me and ask for any advice or counsel I might have had as they worked to navigate their way along this postfaith journey. Eventually I started receiving messages from people around the world on an almost daily basis.

And that's when I began to wonder if I had stumbled into something more definitive of what my next years would encompass. It was also around this time that I joined the board of directors at The Clergy Project. Today I've been given the joy of serving as president, but back then I started off as its communications director. I was having a blast, getting really involved and meeting scores of exciting new faces and friends from other various projects and secular organizations. But more than anything, I really just loved this idea of being able to come alongside others to help them navigate their next steps through this human experience that we all shared together. In a way, it was kind of like the best and most empowering parts of being a pastor.

I've experimented with a lot of other endeavors over the last few years. Everything from business-to-business sales to driving for Uber. I've been a website rater, a company namer, and a jingle slinger. Then there was the day I got to carry a gun on the set of *Chicago P.D.* My mom DVRed the episode, and I wouldn't be surprised if she's still forcing all her friends to watch it.

In early 2015, someone said I should consider becoming a life coach. At first I laughed at the idea. Whatever your suspicions of such characters might be, mine were probably worse to the tenfold. But the more I thought about it, the more I realized how much a pastor and a good coach often share in common. *And who knows*, I thought, *if it could help me make a postfaith living, why not?*

Well, I'm not sure it's helped me make that living just yet, but I completed a life and career coaching certification with an International Coach Federation–accredited training center in San Diego. Though the arsenal of tools I received might not have transformed me into the next Tony Robbins, it's sure made me more effective in partnering with others to help them accomplish their postfaith goals—whether through The Clergy Project, Next Level Coaching, HumanistCoach.com, or all the other little spheres of life. And what was true of me as a pastor is true of me today: I simply want to help others embrace the *truest* version of themselves and to then become the *greatest* version of themselves, with or without all the god stuff.

Basically, I just want to keep doing what I've *always* kept doing. I just want to help my fellow humans make much of life. Individually and in community. Both locally and globally. To successfully navigate life's many obstacles and to transition from religious life to the secular with as little flying shrapnel as possible. By no means does this earthen landscape provide an easy existence, but it can and should be a good one nonetheless. And a joyful one at that. One filled with the wonder of each day's potential. And if I can increase the joy and sanity and happiness and meaningfulness of a few handfuls of people over the course of my life, then I will have considered it a life well lived.

And that right there is what I'd like to call my humble humanist ideal.

And So That's the Story

The thing with stories is that we all have one. Or maybe we all have several actually. We all have a backstory, or even several backstories. We all have a story that we find ourselves currently actively playing within. And we have a story that continues into the future.

Whether you like to think of all those individual stories as chapters or episodes or even entire volumes in and of themselves, they interweave together to create the larger story of our entire lives. That's the big story we're each living out individually. *Our biography of sorts.*

This has been my story. Or at least, it's been the chapters of my story thus far.

And I suppose that my story is now also your story, if for no other reason than that your story includes you reading mine. But when you take all our individual plotlines stretching out around the globe and throughout history, I suppose you could say that together we tell the epic and ever-unfolding story of humanity.

I have to wonder if my sliver of that bigger and more epic story bears any reflection of the rise and fall of belief within the whole of humanity itself. I'm just a small player and not asking for undue attention. And certainly not any credit. I just wonder if we find ourselves in the midst of what might be called a trend. But not the trendy kind of trend. Rather the deadly serious and fundamentally redefining sort of trend. And if I'm just one of many pieces gravitating toward the next logical step in human development.

Or not.

Either way, we find ourselves in the midst of a story. The story of humanity. And thank you for taking time to consider how my story might be folded up within that one.

Now maybe it's time for you to tell yours. At least consider honestly reflecting on it. For those who feel ready and comfortable, consider sharing it with close friends and family members whom you can trust. And then you might find yourself wanting to share it even more widely. To even shout it to the world. And if you want, you can share it with me—*and the world*—by visiting HumanistCoach. com/ShareYourStory. For the sake of dialogue. For the sake of our progression. For your own sake and collectively for all of ours.

Yours might include boldly declaring your atheism.

Or your embrace of a reasonable Christianity.

Or it might simply feature the silent introspection of your own conclusions a little more freely.

But whatever their exact content, our stories continue. As does the epic story of humanity's whole. And it's in service to that story that we will do well to engage in greater conversation with one another. That's the real heartbeat that reverberates from the beginning of this book straight through to its very end.

So the conversation certainly doesn't need to stop here. In fact, we must do what we can to keep it going, for the good progression of all humanity. And it's for this reason that our final chapter addresses this very thing. The need for dialogue. Especially dialogue with those whom we might rather not be dialoguing with. They're human too. And they're worth it.

Questions for the Dialogue

Do we have time for a few more questions? Oh, I'm sure we do.

For Believing Christians

- Do you think it's possible for someone to live a more joy-filled life apart from Christian faith? How so? Would you describe yourself as joyful? What changes in your life do you think would lead you to even greater joy?

- What do you think of the concept described here as humanism? How does it correspond with your impressions of atheism? How do the goals and ideals of a secular humanist differ from your own? How are they similar?

For Atheists and Skeptics

- Why do you think some people are surprised to hear of a believing evangelical pastor who claims to be a humanist? Do you find it surprising? How so? What kind of differences would there have to be between a secular humanist and a Christian humanist? What kind of similarities?

- Have you ever felt alone in your disbelief? How important is it to provide resources of support for the secular community? What kinds of resources would be helpful for those from a religious background who are now attempting to transition to a postfaith lifestyle? What kinds of resources would you like to see available? What can you do to help make them available to others?

Chapter Fourteen

But We're Just Getting Started:
Seven Keys to Keep the Conversation Going

So as I said at the end of the previous chapter, my hope is to keep the conversation going. The end of this book certainly doesn't have to mark the end of the dialogue as a whole. May it rather serve as a transition to an enhanced continuation of it.

And so with all this in mind, I leave you with Seven Keys to Keep the Conversation Going.

Yes, it may be possible to just yell at those you disagree with, but that isn't real dialogue, is it? No, that's a dead conversation, murdered in a blood-boiling rage of frustration and condemnation. Whether you believe in supernatural beings or not makes no difference. Yelling isn't something that convinces others of anything. It's polarizing rather than uniting. It simply renders humanity into further fragments rather than moving us forward as a together-thriving civilization.

No, it's conversation that we want. Real, legitimate, two-way, open and honest yet passionate and driven conversation. And it starts here.

1. Keep an Open Invitation.

It's always tempting to converse only with those who think and feel just as we do, to stick to the same demographics and categories of thought. In fact, sometimes we're instructed to do that by our demographic category leaders. We're told it's safer that way. Fraternize with the enemy and you'll become one.

But for those who are interested in real human progress of thought beyond clichéd assumptions and cognitive comforts, this is never enough. And maybe the fact that you've gotten this far in this book signals your willingness and desire to continue thinking new things in new ways.

The best way to do this is to keep the dialogue open. Be in discussion with those not like you. Read their books and blogs. Listen to their podcasts. Engage with them over coffee or a beer. Include their views and voices in your Facebook feed, and refuse to unfollow a friend just because their politics or religious convictions test or taunt your own.

Even when red flags come up. Red flags can signify that you're getting to substantive issues. In such cases it might mean your assumptions and presumptions are about to be challenged. But that's kind of the whole point of dialoguing with others, right? Hang in there and breathe deep. You'll be okay. And actually, you'll probably be even better than the okay you've previously been comfortable with.

2. Try Not to Assume the Worst in Others.

Maybe it's possible that other people have good reasons for thinking the way they do. Remember that just as you've seen and experienced things that they have not, so they've seen and experienced things that you have not. So maybe—*just maybe*—they've got good reason for approaching life a little differently than you do. And maybe that doesn't automatically render them the bobble-headed dimwit your assumptions have made them out to be.

Let's try not to assume that just because they've come to a different set of answers, they must be evil or stupid or corrosive or a waste of time. Let's extend one another the benefit of the doubt on these things. Just as you'd like them to do the same with you.

Now maybe they will eventually give us good personalized reasons to conclude that, yes, in fact, they are evil or stupid or a corrosive waste of time, and if so, we will handle them accordingly. *What's the old proverb about how if I get fooled again it's my own damn fault?* So yes, let's feel free to apply that old proverb with precision. But let's also refrain from automatically assuming such labels simply because of someone's default perspectives or convictions on an issue.

In order to further and faster stretch our human understanding, let's put down the trash talk and the mean-spirited rhetoric, the shits-and-giggles trolling, and the blatant character assassinations. Let's stop assuming the worst of our opposing categories simply because they believe or disbelieve in ways similar or dissimilar to ourselves. Let's extend the benefit of the doubt and have conversations of substance.

3. Allow Everyone the Space to Think for Themselves.

Skeptics might find it hard to believe, but even evangelicals tend to be ardent defenders of the need to think for oneself, stemming again from that idea of God's Holy Spirit dwelling within you and personally guiding you into all truth. Baptists realized early on that since different religious traditions have different ideas on truth, we need to create space where everyone is allowed to disagree for the moment while everyone thinks for themselves—with or without God's direction.

Freethought—and what it means to be a freethinker—speaks of one's ability to "go wherever the evidence leads," to roam and move and navigate uninhibited across the philosophical, intellectual, and otherwise cognitive canvas, to follow one's urgings regardless of the positions and pressures of other humans and outside forces. And as understandings of how observation, experiential reality, and consciousness continue to grow and develop, we will do well to keep in mind that not everyone will come to the same conclusions that we do. And this should be okay.

Indeed, freethought calls each of us not only to advocate for our own ability to think independently, but also to advocate for the freethought of others, even when—*and maybe even especially when*—they disagree with our own personal conclusions. To fight for one's own nonreligious views while denying others the right to disagree is not true freethought. It's simply ideological arrogance and bullying.

Besides, demanding others into agreement only changes external claims, not true convictions. If anything, when one demands the agreement of others, it often makes its victims even more determined to retain previous viewpoints than they were before.

No, the best thing to do is to allow others to disagree. Provide them the breathing room to think for themselves. Maintain a calm and peaceable dialogue. And maybe in time, they will come around to your way of thinking. Or maybe you will come around to theirs. But either way, our best chances for clear and reasoned thinking are sabotaged when we attempt to force or demand allegiance, regardless of whether it's in favor of religion or in critique against it.

4. Passionately Argue Your Strongest Positions.

The previous point is not to say you ought just lie down and let people continue in ignorance. After all, you likely came to your current position precisely because you've thought long and hard about it and are closer to an accurate understanding than you were a few years ago.

I'm extending you the benefit of the doubt, you see . . . ;)

In the marketplace of ideas, we want to see the highest quality merchandise available. This pertains to ideas from every realm of theory, from the underpinnings of the universe itself to political ideology, from a spanning range of philosophy to, yes, religious speculations. We want to see the greatest merchandise available. The only way we can have confidence in our own positions is if we've truly weighed them against the greatest positions of others. And this allows us to sharpen and fine-tune our own ideas and perspectives in the process.

When done well, the entire marketplace feeds off itself in the healthiest of ways as we truly approach one another in the collective quest for progress. Unfortunately, not everyone approaches the dialogue in such healthy ways, but even as they might be left behind as a result, the rest of us find ourselves better equipped to move forward. And hopefully one day the remaining segment will catch up. We will push forward nonetheless.

But this requires that we each offer our best ideas with the strongest defense possible. And that we do so publicly. It's critical to realize that publicly articulating one's perspective—*and even passionately so*—does not indicate arrogance or an attempt at philosophical dictatorship. At least not the inherent act itself of speaking loudly and passionately. No, since such a defense can benefit the public conversation, it must be viewed as a good thing, a constructive thing, a progressive thing. It is in my best interest that you bring me your best arguments. And it is in your best interest that I offer you the same in return.

But this is where we must grow slow to feel offended when we hear public disagreements with our positions. It is for our own good that we hear things we disagree with. And we must remember that a less than full articulation of the other side robs us of the opportunity to truly sharpen our own perspectives and even possibly move beyond them. But either way, a fully loaded and passionately invigorated marketplace of ideas will inevitably offer some of those ideas that contrast with our own. And this is a good thing, a healthy thing, a progressive thing.

At least it can be. But this is where however loud and passionately we offer our perspectives, we can and must still offer them in humility. Let me provide you the best evidence for what I'm convinced of even as I admit that my perspective is continually evolving and adapting and that I might be wrong on some things. But I nonetheless offer them with the greatest of vigor, doing so even as I invite you to give me your best swing of response in return. Together we battle with the best of intentions so that a greater and higher level of understanding and perspective may result.

I realize, of course, that the vast majority of people do not engage one another this way. Not in the least. Usually it's one of these two half-alternatives: either, one, we misconstrue humility as indifference and avoid all passionate conversation entirely, or, two, we pervert our passion into an arrogance that refuses others even the ability to speak without interruption. But the key, however, is to hold them together. In balance. To argue passionately yet respectfully, at length but in turn.

And to do so over food and drink always helps. It helps remind us of our humanity and the context of community within which we function.

The key is to in a sense say, *This is my greatest articulation for where I'm at—and I really and truly believe this is the best stance I've seen thus far—but I am nonetheless continually open for the revisal of my own positions.*

So yes, argue and defend, engage and contend. Do it loudly, do it vigorously, and give it your best shot. But do it with civility, humility, and calm. And remember to give them the benefit of the doubt until they've personally proven it to no longer apply. Even then remain calm and collected while moving on to new conversations.

5. Always Make Time to be Honest.

First with yourself. Let's take time to be honest with ourselves. To really consider why we believe what we believe, to trace out what led us to the conclusions we currently hold. And we want to consider the possibility that our positions may be held simply because they are comfortable or familiar. Maybe we hold to what we hold to simply because we've built our entire lives around such concepts and can't handle the idea of it all being for naught. Maybe it's because we've even built careers on such beliefs and taught them to others and we just can't bear the thought of having to eat crow and take them all back. Or maybe it's because we truly and *honestly* believe to have the best answers currently available given our own personal experiences, observations, and study. Even more important than knowing the content of our positions might be knowing where they come from and the biases that inform them.

And then also with others. We need to also be honest with those around us. Don't worry about eating crow. This is a community endeavor, and if our friends around us are also humble, they'll simply be thankful for our humility and honesty. But let's get real. And let's push envelopes.

6. Be Bold in the Push for More.

Honestly, who cares what others think or how they'll react. Let's keep up the search for greater discoveries and the deepest of truths. And let's get real about it. Let's push and pull the most magnificent work and ideas and theories and research out of one another. Yes, some might castigate you for going beyond artificial or arbitrary boundaries created by those who have no business doing so. Some might cut you off and disassociate with you. You might lose some friendships. But there will be new ones. Let's push forward. Let's think critically and hypothesize liberally. Let's learn and advance and teach and listen. Let's make it happen, and let's do it together.

7. Celebrate Even in Disagreement.

There is so much wonder and joy in this life! And it's even better when it's enjoyed together. Yes, let's debate and contend and make proclamations from marketplace booths. That's all well and good even on its own, but let's then take time to set the debate aside and bring a meaning to this life that extends beyond our camps of belief and ideology. May family gatherings, neighborhood barbeques, and community service initiatives never be smothered by an inability to take disagreement in stride. When we share our common humanity, sometimes that's all that should matter.

So yes, let's know when to step away from the marketplace and into a fresh steam of splendid sunshine.

Let's go to the beach and share picnics in the park.

Let's go on spontaneous adventures and then turn on our music and blast it loudly.

Let's partner together with one another to rake leaves and build gazebos.

Is this stuff just ridiculously optimistic and stupidly fluffy? I don't know but let's find ways to get lost in the wonder of the whole damn thing. And let's learn to enjoy it once in awhile.

So let's raise our children to marvel at the wonders all around us.

Every blade of grass and each rock that can be skipped across the surface of a pond.

The chipmunk that scampers along the backyard fence.

The long neck of a giraffe.

The humans that live in Argentina along with those in Mongolia and India and France.

Hemmingway and Poe.

Monet and Pollack.

Jazz and Swing.

Capra and the Coens.

Bike lanes and skate parks.

History museums and threshing shows.

Birthday parties and graduations.

Let's make each moment count and savor every breath in our lungs.

Let's celebrate the wonder of community along the landscape of our lives.

And let's do it *together*.

I trust that this is the stuff that makes all our conversations and inquiries and quests for insight worthwhile. This is what makes them meaningful. This is what colors them with depth and richness. For it's these moments and wonders and a long line of others like them that make each of us and the story we share unmistakably *human*.

We're winding down now. And I confess I don't have all the answers. I've never claimed to. If I did, I guess that would make me God. But I don't, so I'm not.

None of us do, and therefore none of us are.

But we do have this earthen community we call humanity.

We do have one another.

And because none of us are all-knowing gods or goddesses, I suspect this makes our human community all the more important, especially in our pursuit of joy and relationship and purpose and, yes, things like knowledge and truth. May we together strive for the furthering of freedom, for the wonder of discovery, and for the riches of one another. May we enhance the majesty of this life in all its love and laughter. May we not limit the collective human experience by forcing on others what we might wish it to have been or to be. May we further it by taking it as it is, engaging in reality, and truly making the most of life in every sphere of our existence. And may we first and foremost and lastly and forever do it together. The conversation is ours. The story is ours. We're all in this *together*.

Questions for the Dialogue

One final set.

For Everyone

- Which of these seven keys do you already practice effortlessly? Which of them are more difficult for you? Are there any that you outright reject?

- Which of these seven keys will you work to grow better at? And what steps will you take to make sure you get better at them in the near future?

- Is there any other key that you might add to the list? If so, why?

Epilogue

You never know it's coming until it's already here. I'm talking about death. Or at least the kind of death that sneaks up on you while you're distracted with the rest of life. And in the summer of 2015, it had indeed snuck up on me. And it almost wasn't caught in time.

In the third week of July I had unknowingly contracted a bacterial infection that would quickly grow quite severe and then rapidly subjugate every corner of my body. But days before any of that terrible bodily subjugation stuff happened, on a Wednesday evening, I had simply felt like I might be coming down with a mere cold.

The following afternoon—Thursday—it had appeared that I might have an inflamed gland. It was quite painful, so I decided to keep an eye on it. But that was about it. I ran off to work for an evening shift at the steakhouse and went about my day.

That evening at work, however, I began to notice some increased swelling and came down with a bit of a fever. As the next couple hours wore on, my clothes grew terribly uncomfortable against my bloating body.

Feeling miserable after work, I made my way home and went right to bed but was kept up tossing and turning throughout the night with a terrible fever.

I woke up Friday morning to discover my swollen body had doubled in size—*literally*. I was overwhelmed with crazy-intense pain and profuse sweating. I stumbled around finding it almost impossible to walk due to extreme disorientation and physical weakness. Not usually one for hospitals or ambulances, I decided to cab it to the local immediate care clinic. But from there, they soon sent me to the local hospital's emergency room.

And there in the emergency room, they discovered a bacterial skin infection that in less than forty-eight hours had made its way into my blood stream. That very afternoon as I was lying in triage, double pneumonia began to set in. They later told me that the infection had stormed so relentlessly through my body that if I had waited just one more day to check myself into the hospital, they most likely would not have been able to save me. During a reevaluation with my infectious-diseases specialist a few months later, it was clarified that had I waited until Saturday, I would have surely died.

Talk about coming out of nowhere. Healthy as possible on Tuesday and potentially Drop-Dead-Fred by Saturday. From a simple skin infection.

This Was Just Crazy.

Needless to say, it took more than a few days to recover. In fact, I carried some of the resulting muscle deterioration for nearly a year afterward. But as you might suspect, my hospital stay became one of those experiences where every day the doctors—or rather, the four different *teams* of specialists—discovered another new ramification of my illness. And in the ongoing discovery of more ramifications, that Monday a test revealed that something more was going on in one of my lungs.

The pulmonary team needed a closer look in order to be sure. But they thought it could be a blood clot, maybe an embolism, maybe something more. We all sat in terrified anticipation as to what a *something-more* might look like. And so they scheduled a CT angiogram for later that day. Then they explained that if the scan's results were to come back unclear, they'd have to run another test in its place. But they didn't want to have to run that other test unless it was absolutely necessary, since it could end up collapsing my lung or something. Basically they just wanted us to stay calm and keep an open mind. Try not to fear the worst.

By this time my parents were with me in Chicago, fearing the worst of the *something-mores*, along with my brother and his fiancée. And of course Justina and the children as well. After the pulmonary scan was scheduled, there was about an hour or so where my family left to run some necessary errands on my behalf while I sat alone in the hospital room.

And it was here where it hit me.

There was no panic, no fear, no anxiety. I was completely calm and collected. I really was. But I had a realization. On top of the fact that I had no idea how bad this thing was going to keep getting and how many more ramifications the doctors would continue discovering, on top of this, I began thinking of the many people I had visited in their own hospital rooms back when I was a pastor. And then I began thinking of the many routine hospital stays I had participated in as a pastor that had quickly spiraled into something much bigger. And then my mind started visiting the rooms of unexpected tragedy, realizing how quickly the routine can indeed escalate to crisis. I was reminded of how fragile human life really is and of how quickly an apparently simple illness can take it all away.

And lying there I wondered, how many people were right now preparing for a simple angiogram and staying positive, thinking life was going to be just fine in a few days, only to discover that tragedy would strike and they would be gone of this world by the end of the week.

Sounds morbid. Maybe terrifying. But as a pastor, you see this kind of thing on the regular. Your mind and heart instinctively prepare for it. I guess even when it's for yourself.

And so I was sitting there in the hospital room. Totally calm and collected. Not fearful or terrified. But wondering what if—*just what if*—something was to go terribly wrong and I were to be dead by the end of the day. And I contemplated that idea for a few minutes. *What if today was the day I was to die? Or the day I was to be beset with a state of unconsciousness that would linger to the day I was to die? What if all my years and experiences had led me to this? To this fateful hospital bed?*

And I asked myself if I could be happy having lived and died like this. I asked myself about regrets and do-overs. I asked myself if I could be okay with it all.

And then I was filled with peace. I decided I was very happy with where my life had brought me. I had no regrets, or at least very few of them, all things considered. Even in the midst of all that I was working toward and of all my goals that yet remained unattained, I nonetheless had accomplished and enjoyed much. And this life is short and not a guarantee, so who was I to demand more than what I had already been abundantly granted. And somehow this produced something of a surge of tranquility.

And I smiled.

There was no panic or hyperventilating. No running around the room in circles.

I smiled and relaxed and closed my eyes knowing that should this just so happen to be my last day on this earth, I had found immense satisfaction in a life well lived. I had done my best and enjoyed the ride.

And then I got up, hobbled around, and found some scratch paper.

I decided that if by chance this might just so happen to be my last of days, I should leave a note behind. After I was done, I hid it way down deep in my take-home bag where I knew no one would look unless things had gone terribly wrong.

Most of the letter was written to my children. I said the same kinds of sentimental things you'd probably say if you had thought you might never see your children again. My words to them were followed by those to several other loved ones.

And then I had something more to say. I said I had no fear of death. I said that I remained confident that there were no gods and no afterlife awaiting me on The Other Side, because there was no Other Side to be awaited by. I apologized for my premature departure, and I encouraged loved ones to do what I had tried to do, to make the most of this life, the one that is actually the only one we really have to live.

I asked them not to worry for me. I told them that though I wasn't spending those potentially final moments crying out to God in prayer, I was using them to reminisce and remember all the good times I'd had with each of them. That I was thankful and currently experiencing a wonderful state of peace and inner comfort. That though I would have loved the opportunity to keep living, I was simply thankful to have lived as long and as full as I had. I shared that as I wrote the letter and even as tears made their way down my cheek, I was smiling and I was overflowing with a groundswell of joy and gratitude and satisfaction.

In other words, I was in the foxhole. I'm guessing we're all well aware of the overstated assertion that *there are no atheists in foxholes*. The claim of course being that in war, every soldier turns to God for safe rescue, and the implication being that regardless of the exact context, when on one's deathbed and facing the imminent pitch-black darkness, *we all* uncover an inner compulsion to finally repent of rebellion and inevitably cry out to the Christian God in prayer. This is because even atheists secretly know the truth of God's reality—because deep down, even they are terrified of the hell they can't completely deny.

And now here I was in that quote-unquote foxhole. And though I didn't *expect* to die, I was well aware of the possibility. And I took planned precautions just in case. But here's the thing. Never for one moment did I consider prayer. I never prayed. Not even one word. I never looked to God. I never reconsidered his existence. I wasn't filled with terror or horror or fear. No anxiety or panic. No dark thoughts or depression. No crazed running around. Nope. Just calm. Peace and calm and savoring every moment of this amazing thing called life. Even alone in a hospital room.

Thankfully, I didn't die. Not yet anyway. But I guess I really am thankful to have almost died. I'm thankful for how it showed me that *this* is real. That *this* is sanity. And that *this* is enough to conquer all my fears and frustrations. It reassured me that I really don't have anything to lose. That in my atheism I'm right where I need to be. And that, no, I really don't need God for any false form of metaphysical strength.

And it confirmed, once again and with even greater strength, something that I've long suspected since the early days of my deconversion.

That I really am more joyful *without* Jesus.

Acknowledgments

This project could not have taken place without the support and partnership of so many incredible individuals. I thank Ray Kadkhodaian, who first encouraged me to begin the therapeutic exercise of journaling my deconversion experience, which eventually turned into this book. I thank John Compere, Linda LaScola, Michael Thomas Tower, Peter Boghossian, and Dan Barker (who also wrote the foreword) for taking time to read manuscript drafts and provide feedback. And of course, I'm ever so thankful for Kurt Volkan, who not only offered invaluable direction throughout this project, but also believed in it enough to bring it to print. What an honor it is to be included in the Pitchstone family!

And this book certainly wouldn't exist had it not been for those who helped shape my story so profoundly. My dear sisters and brothers at The Clergy Project came alongside me when I needed them most. I thank Scott Schupbach for bringing me to the Moody Heretics, and I thank that heretic Lana Wood for then pointing me toward The Clergy Project. *I wouldn't even be here without you two!* Terry Plank, thank you for your tireless leadership as The Clergy Project's first president, for your years of support and encouragement to me personally, and for your ongoing guidance and friendship. Teresa MacBain, thank you for helping me feel right at home, and I wish you well with your return to Christian belief and in all your future endeavors. Dave Warnock and John Compere, thank you for being true brothers to me. Linda LaScola, thank you for your invaluable partnership and support on so many fronts. Dan Dennett, you are a truly heartwarming joy. And Dan Barker, thank you for all you've given both to The Clergy Project and to me personally. The return on your labors is beyond measure.

I thank West Hills Community Church and Bethel Community Church for helping me discover what true community looks like—complete with rolled-up sleeves and shoulders to lean on. Mike Gugliuzza, thank you for reconnecting to do the Moody interview and for your ongoing support. Rob Bukowski and Jim LaBorn, thank you for your years of unending friendship and partnership in all things church and beyond.

Mom and Dad, thank you for your unending love and encouragement even in times that may have been less than easy. You've always given your absolute best, and the joys I carry from my childhood are many. Mike, you remain a highlight of every trip back home—thank you for being my brother.

Justina, so much of this journey was *our* journey. You were there for me even when I wasn't there for myself. And so many times, you held me together when I couldn't even stand. You were my sanity. We created a beautiful family together, we will always be partners, and I still consider you among my closest friends. *We've got this.*

Janett and Jocelyn, *who would I be without you?* As I've said many countless times, you *are* my life. Among my greatest privileges has been watching you two grow and develop as the amazing individuals you've become, and I'm thrilled to see where life takes both of you in the years and decades ahead. Just be yourselves and be them confidently, and nothing can stop you! You push me to greatness every single day, and my overflowing joy in life has been being your father.

Resources

For Assessing One's Faith in Light of Reality

Armstrong, Karen. *A History of God: The 4000-Year Quest of Judaism, Christianity, and Islam*. New York: Random House, 2011.

Barker, Dan. *God: The Most Unpleasant Character in All Fiction*. New York: Sterling, 2016.

———. *Godless: How an Evangelical Preacher Became One of America's Leading Atheists*. Berkeley: Ulysses: 2008.

Dawkins, Richard. *The God Delusion*. New York: Harcourt, 2006.

———. *The Selfish Gene*. New York: Oxford University Press, 1976.

Dennett, Daniel C. *Breaking the Spell: Religion as a Natural Phenomenon*. New York: Penguin: 2006.

Dennett, Daniel C. and Linda LaScola. *Caught in the Pulpit: Leaving Belief Behind*, expanded and updated ed. Durham, NC: Pitchstone, 2015.

González, Justo L. *The Story of Christianity. Volume 1: The Early Church to the Dawn of Reformation*. New York: HarperCollins, 1984.

———. *The Story of Christianity. Volume 2: The Reformation to the Present Day*. New York: Harper Collins, 1985.

Harris, Sam. *The End of Faith: Religion, Terror, and the Future of Reason*. New York: Norton, 2004.

Hitchens, Christopher. *God Is Not Great: How Religion Poisons Everything*. New York: Twelve, 2007.

Jacoby, Susan. *Strange Gods: A Secular History of Conversion*. New York: Vintage, 2017.

Krauss, Lawrence M. *The Greatest Story Ever Told—So Far: Why Are We Here?* New York: Atria, 2017.

———. *A Universe from Nothing: Why There Is Something Rather than Nothing*. New York: Atria, 2013.

Navabi, Armin. *Why There Is No God: Simple Responses to 20 Common Arguments for the Existence of God*. Vancouver: Atheist Republic, 2014.

Nye, Bill. *Undeniable: Evolution and the Science of Creation*. New York: St. Martin's, 2014.

Prothero, Stephen. *God Is Not One: The Eight Rival Religions That Run the World—and Why Their Differences Matter*. New York: HarperCollins, 2010.

———. *Religious Literacy: What Every American Needs to Know—and Doesn't*. New York: HarperCollins, 2008.

Russell, Bertrand. *Why I Am Not a Christian and Other Essays on Religion and Related Subjects*. New York: Simon & Schuster, 1957.

Swenson, Kristin. *Bible Babel: Making Sense of the Most Talked About Book of All Time*. New York: HarperCollins, 2010.

Tarnas, Richard. *The Passion of the Western Mind: Understanding the Ideas That Have Shaped Our World View*. New York: Ballantine, 1991.

For Building a Life Beyond Faith

Barker, Dan. *Life Driven Purpose: How an Atheist Finds Meaning*. Durham, NC: Pitchstone, 2015.

Campolo, Tony and Bart Campolo. *Why I Left, Why I Stayed: Conversations on Christianity Between an Evangelical Father and His Humanist Son*. New York: HarperOne, 2017.

Christina, Greta. *Comforting Thoughts About Death That Have Nothing to Do with God*. Durham, NC: Pitchstone, 2015.

————. *Coming Out Atheist: How to Do It, How to Help Each Other, and Why.* Durham, NC: Pitchstone, 2014.

————. *The Way of the Heathen: Practicing Atheism in Everyday Life.* Durham, NC: Pitchstone, 2016.

Epstein, Greg. *Good Without God: What a Billion Nonreligious People Do Believe.* New York: HarperCollins, 2010.

Gorham, Candace R. M. *The Ebony Exodus Project: Why Some Black Women Are Walking Out on Religion—and Others Should Too.* Durham, NC: Pitchstone, 2014.

Gottschall, Jonathan. *The Storytelling Animal: How Stories Make Us Human.* New York: Mariner, 2013.

Haley, Jeff T. and Dale McGowan. *Sharing Reality: How to Bring Secularism and Science to an Evolving Religious World.* Durham, NC: Pitchstone, 2017.

Jacoby, Susan. *Freethinkers: A History of American Secularism.* New York: Metropolitan, 2004.

McGowan, Dale. *In Faith and in Doubt: How Religious Believers and Nonbelievers Can Create Strong Marriages and Loving Families.* New York: American Management Association, 2014.

————, ed. *Parenting Beyond Belief: On Raising Ethical, Caring Kids Without Religion.* New York: American Management Association, 2009.

Noise, David. *Nonbeliever Nation: The Rise of Secular Americans.* New York: St. Martin's, 2012.

Ozment, Katherine. *Grace Without God: The Search for Meaning, Purpose, and Belonging in a Secular Age.* New York: HarperCollins, 2016.

Ray, Darrell. *God & Sex: How Religion Distorts Sexuality.* Kansas City: IPC Press, 2012.

Russell, Wendy Thomas. *Relax, It's Just God: How and Why to Talk to Your Kids About Religion When You're not Religious.* Long Beach, CA: Brown Paper, 2015.

Vosper, Gretta. *Amen: What Prayer Can Mean in a World Beyond Belief.* New York: HarperCollins, 2014.

————. *With or Without God: Why the Way We Live is More Important Than What We Believe.* New York: HarperCollins, 2008.

Zimmerman, Phil. *Living the Secular Life: New Answers to Old Questions*. New York: Penguin, 2015.

For Gaining Insights from the Stories of Others

Alcántar, Fernando. *To the Cross and Back: An Immigrant's Journey from Faith to Reason*. Durham, NC: Pitchstone, 2015.

Andrews, Seth. *Deconverted: A Journey from Religion to Reason*. Denver: Outskirts, 2012.

Barker, Dan. *Godless: How an Evangelical Preacher Became One of America's Leading Atheists*. Berkeley: Ulysses: 2008.

———. *Losing Faith in Faith: From Preacher to Atheist*. Madison: Freedom From Religion Foundation, 2006.

Batchelor, Stephen. *Confession of a Buddhist Atheist*. New York: Spiegel & Grau, 2011.

Compere, John S. *Outgrowing Religion: Why a Fifth-Generation Southern Baptist Minister Left God for Good*. (n.p.): John S. Compere Publishing, 2016. Originally published as *Towards the Light: A Fifth Generation Baptist Minister's Journey from Religion to Reason*.

DeWitt, Jerry. *Hope After Faith: An Ex-Pastor's Journey from Belief to Atheism*. Boston: DeCapo, 2013.

Dunphy, Catherine. *From Apostle to Apostate: The Story of The Clergy Project*. Durham, NC: Pitchstone, 2015.

Johnson, Mary. *An Unquenchable Thirst: A Memoir*. New York: Spiegel & Grau, 2013.

Kenneally, Marion. *One Nun's Odyssey: A Memoir*. Denver: Outskirts, 2016.

Lobdell, William. *Losing my Religion: How I Lost My Faith Reporting on Religion in American and Found Unexpected Peace*. New York: Harper, 2009.

Pinn, Anthony. *Writing God's Obituary: How a Good Methodist Became a Better Atheist*. Amherst: Prometheus, 2014.

Uhl, Stephen Frederick. *Out of God's Closet: This Priest Psychologist Chooses Friendly Atheism*. Indianapolis: Golden Rule Publishing, 2009.

About the Author

Drew Bekius is a man of many loves: people, community, sanity, adventure, human potential, personality type, team dynamics, a good challenge, a mighty comeback story, a hearty laugh, irreverent comedy, those brave enough to tell it like it is, those confident enough to put him in his place, a rich Sumatra roast, a generous pour of Highland Park neat, a great walk along the lakeshore on a breezy summer day, an audacity to change the world.

Drew is a personal coach and the creator of HumanistCoach.com. A former pastor, he serves as president of The Clergy Project and is endorsed as a humanist celebrant by The Humanist Society. He is the author of *Your Next Life Now* and blogs occasionally at DrewBekius.com. Drew has two amazing daughters and lives in Uptown, Chicago.